William Richard Morfill

Simplified grammar of the Serbian language

William Richard Morfill

Simplified grammar of the Serbian language

ISBN/EAN: 9783337085568

Printed in Europe, USA, Canada, Australia, Japan

Cover: Foto ©Paul-Georg Meister /pixelio.de

More available books at **www.hansebooks.com**

TRÜBNER'S COLLECTION

OF

SIMPLIFIED GRAMMARS

OF THE PRINCIPAL

ASIATIC AND EUROPEAN LANGUAGES.

EDITED BY

REINHOLD ROST, LL.D., PH.D.

XVI.

SERBIAN.

By W. R. MORFILL, M.A.

TRÜBNER'S COLLECTION OF SIMPLIFIED GRAMMARS OF THE PRINCIPAL ASIATIC AND EUROPEAN LANGUAGES.

EDITED BY REINHOLD ROST, LL.D., PH.D.

I.
HINDUSTANI, PERSIAN AND ARABIC. By the late E. H. Palmer, M.A. *Second Edition. Price 5s.*

II.
HUNGARIAN. By I. Singer. *Price 4s. 6d.*

III.
BASQUE. By W. Van Eys. *Price 3s. 6d.*

IV.
MALAGASY. By G. W. Parker. *Price 5s.*

V.
MODERN GREEK. By E. M. Geldart, M.A. *Price 2s. 6d.*

VI.
ROUMANIAN. By R. Torceanu. *Price 5s.*

VII.
TIBETAN. By H. A. Jaschke. *Price 5s.*

VIII.
DANISH. By E. C. Otté. *Price 2s. 6d.*

IX.
OTTOMAN TURKISH. By J. W. Redhouse. *Price 10s. 6d.*

X.
SWEDISH. By E. C. Otté. *Price 2s. 6d.*

XI.
POLISH. By W. R. Morfill, M.A. *Price 3s. 6d.*

XII.
PALI. By Edward Müller, LL.D. *Price 7s. 6d.*

XIII.
SANSKRIT. By Hjalmar Edgren, Ph.D. *Price 10s. 6d.*

XIV.
ALBANIAN. By P. W. *Price 7s. 6d.*

XV.
JAPANESE. By B. H. Chamberlain. *Price 5s.*

XVI.
SERBIAN. By W. R. Morfill, M.A. *Price 4s. 6d.*

Grammars of the following are in preparation:—
Anglo-Saxon, Assyrian, Bohemian, Bulgarian, Burmese, Chinese, Cymric and Gaelic, Dutch, Egyptian, Finnish, Hebrew, Khassi, Kurdish, Malay, Russian, Siamese, Singhalese, &c. &c.

London: TRÜBNER & CO., Ludgate Hill.

SIMPLIFIED GRAMMAR

OF THE

SERBIAN LANGUAGE

BY

W. R. MORFILL, M. A.

LONDON:
TRÜBNER & Co., LUDGATE HILL
1887.

PREFACE.

The object of the Serbian grammar now laid before the public is to give a short account of the chief characteristics of the language. It is believed that these will be found adequately stated, although with great brevity. I have derived some assistance from the grammar of A. PARČIĆ, of which a French translation has appeared(¹) but in the classification of the nouns and verbs have followed MIKLOSICH (Vergleichende Grammatik) and DANIČIĆ (Облици Српскога Језика, 3rd edition, Belgrade 1863). The grammatical forms in this little work are treated throughout in such a way as to bring the language in harmony with those of the Old Slavonic, its eldest surviving sister. It is only upon such principles that they can be properly explained.

In treating a language where so many dialects struggle for supremacy, it has been impossible to avoid a certain amount of inconsistency in orthography and grammatical forms, but I have taken pains that all the most prominent variations should be noted. Although the basis of the

---

(¹) Grammaire de la langue Serbo-Croate par A. PARČIĆ. Paris 1877. The translation is by M. J. B. FEUVRIER who dates his preface from Cetinje, the capital of Tsrnagora (Montenegro). For proper names I use the Croatian orthography but retain the more familiar form of that of MIKLOSICH.

little work has been the Serbian language in the stricter sense of the term, it has not been found practicable to exclude Croatisms, considering the great importance of Agram as a literary centre and the merit of the authors who have used that dialect. Owing to the Old Slavonic as modified by Serbisms, having been the book-language till nearly the close of the first thirty years of this century the *sermo vulgaris* has hardly had time to fully develop itself. The orthography has fluctuated greatly and the modifications of the Cyrillic alphabet introduced by VUK only came into general use in Serbia in 1868.

I have treated the accents but briefly. My own experience, corroborated by the opinion of Serbs themselves has told me that it is impossible to represent by any words these striking combinations of stress and tone. They can only be acquired orally.[1] The Serbs employ them but little either in writing or printing.

The following details of the area over which the Serbo-Croatian language is spoken will be found useful.

According to the latest statistics it is the vernacular of about seven millions, who are distributed over the following territories:

1) The kingdom of Serbia,
2) The part of Old Serbia still under Turkish rule,
3) Bosnia and Herzegovina,
4) Istria, the Dalmatian littoral and the islands,
5) The Principality of Montenegro,

---

[1] Bošković in his grammar (Theoretisch-Praktisches Lehrbuch zur Erlernung der serbischen Sprache. Pest, 1864), has given a musical notation to help the student.

6) The Austrian Provinces: Croatia, Slavonia, Syrmia and the southern part of Carniola,

7) The Serbs in the Banat and South-Hungary,

8) A few who are settled in the South of Russia.

Those of this people who adhere to the Greek church use the Cyrillic alphabet; those who follow the Roman catholic rite the Latin. In some parts of Dalmatia there is used in the Church-books the strange alphabet called Glagolitic, about the origin and age of which so much has been written, but up to the present time with little result. One point only seems to have been proved, namely that it is older than Cyrillic. Closely connected with the Serbian language is the Slovenish spoken by about a million and a half of people, in Carinthia and parts of Styria and Carniola. About forty years ago an attempt was made by Dr. LJUDEVIT GÁJ of Agram to form a literary language by fusing Slovenish and Serbo-Croatian, but his effects were not successful. The *jus et norma loquendi* do not depend upon scholars or journalists and the artificial tongue which he essayed to create would have been unintelligible to the humbler classes. Nay, the establishment of such a language would only have defeated the main object of this warm-hearted and patriotic enthusiast. It would have paved the way for the complete Germanisation of the country. Slovenish, a most interesting language, has accordingly gone on its own path. An excellent grammar by ŠUMAN, a pupil of MIKLOSICH has recently been published at the expense of the *Matica Slovenska* of Laibach.([1]) Although Serbo-Croatian literat-

---

([1]) Slovenska Slovnica po Miklošičevi primerjalni. V Ljubljani 1882.

ure (as opposed to old Slavonic texts in Serbian recensions) is of comparatively modern origin, yet the reader will find much to reward him in the writings of STANKO VRAZ, RADIČEVIĆ, PRERADOVIĆ and BAN, to say nothing of the fine collections of popular ballads many of which are probably of great antiquity. The Serbian Review Гласник (Messenger), published periodically at Belgrade contains a large number of articles on the literature and history of the country, by such men as GJURO DANIČIĆ, STOJAN NOVAKOVIĆ, ČEDOMIL MIJATOVIĆ([1]) and others. At the time of his premature death DANIČIĆ was engaged in the preparation of a large Serbo-Croatian dictionary which is now being continued by his pupils. It will probably take rank with the Polish work of LINDE and the Chekh of JUNGMANN.—In conclusion I may add that the present grammar is the first attempt to familiarise Englishmen with the principles of the Serbian language, and I must return my hearty thanks to Mr. ALEXANDER Z. JOVIČIĆ (Secretary of the Serbian legation in London), for the kindness and care with which he has looked over the proofs and the interest he has taken in the work throughout.

OXFORD
1887.

W. R. MORFILL.

([1]) To his Excellency ČEDOMIL MIJATOVIĆ formerly Serbian Minister to the court of St. James and now Serbian Minister of Finance I am under great obligations for allowing me to submit to his criticism the sheets of this work while passing through the press, amidst his many avocations. He must not however be held responsible for their contents.

CONTENTS

Part I:—Phonology.

	page
The alphabet	1
The accents	4
Characteristics of the dialects	8

Part II:—Doctrine of Forms.

The gender of substantives	11
Declension: ъ (*a*)-stems	12
o-stems and a-stems	14
ъ (*u*)-stems and ь-stems	15
Consonantal stems: в, н, с	16
т, р	17
Adjectives	19
Degrees of comparison	22
The numerals	23
Pronouns	24
The reflexive pronoun	25
Demonstrative pronouns	27
The Verb	30
Prefixes	33
Stems without suffixes	35
nq-stems	41
ê-stems	42
i-stems	44

VIII CONTENTS.

a-stems
ova (*na*)-stems
Compound tenses
The verb бити
Paradigm of a complete verb
The passive voice
Irregular verbs
Adverbs
Prepositions
Conjunctions
Interjections

Part III:—Syntax.

The noun
The verb
Serbian reading lesson

Part I:—PHONOLOGY.

The Serbian language will be treated in this Grammar as more or less identical with the Croatian. According as this language is spoken by Serbs or Croats it employs the Cyrillic or Latin Alphabet.—For the former the system adopted by Vuk Stephanovich Karajich is now generally used, and for the latter the modified forms introduced by Ljudevit Gaj.

CYRILLIAN PRINTED AND CURSIVE	LATIN		PRONUNCIATION
А а	A a	A a	a Italian
Б б	B b	B b	b
В в	V v	V v	v
Г г	G g	G g	g always hard
Д д	D d	D d	d
Ђ ђ	Dj, Gj, dj, gj	Dj, Gj, dj, gj	dy
Е е	E e	E e	e Italian
Ж ж	Ž ž	Ž ž	j French jour
З з	Z z	Z z	z
И и	I i	I i	i

A

SERBIAN GRAMMAR.

CYRILLIAN PRINTED AND CURSIVE		LATIN				PRONUNCIATION
J j	*J j*	J	j	*J*	*j*	y
K к	*K k k*	K	k	*K*	*k*	k
Л л	*L L l*	L	l	*L*	*l*	l
Љ љ	*Lj Lj*	Lj	lj	*Lj*	*lj*	lj Italian gl
M м	*M m*	M	m	*M*	*m*	m
Н н	*N N n*	N	n	*N*	*n*	n
Њ њ	*Nj Nj*	Nj	nj	*Nj*	*nj*	gn French
О о	*O O o*	O	o	*O*	*o*	o
П п	*P P p*	P	p	*P*	*p*	p
Р р	*R R r*	R	r	*R*	*r*	r
С с	*S S s*	S	s	*S*	*s*	s
Т т	*T T m*	T	t	*T*	*t*	t
Ћ ћ	*Ć ć*	Ć	ć	*Ć*	*ć*	between ch and ts
У у	*U U u*	U	u	*U*	*u*	ou French
Ф ф	*F F f*	F	f	*F*	*f*	f
Х х	*H H h*	H	h	*H*	*h*	German ch as *machen*
Ц ц	*C C c*	C	c	*C*	*c*	ts
Ч ч	*Č č*	Č	č	*Č*	*č*	ch as in *church*
Џ џ	*Dž dž*	Dž	dž	*Dž*	*dž*	dzh = Engl. j
Ш ш	*Š š*	Š	š	*Š*	*š*	sh

These are the alphabets now in ordinary use as previously stated. I have not thought it necessary to give any others, which would probably only bewilder the reader. It is to be regretted that religious reasons still cause a separation in the alphabets employed by the Serbs and Croats; the former belonging to the Greek church use the Cyrillic, the latter as Roman Catholics the Latin. It is almost ludicrous to see works partly printed in one alphabet and partly in the other. Thus in the Magazine 'Slovinac' which appeared at Ragusa in 1878 and subsequent years we have frequently one column in Cyrillic and one in Latin letters. The letter џ is considered by MIKLOSICH as superfluous (Comp. Gram. I. 412). It is however of use in words derived from Turkish, many of which are still to be found in the Serbian language. He speaks of it as derived from the Roumanian, but according to SHAFARIK (Serbische Lesekörner p. 63), it had previously been used in Serbian in the seventeenth century.

The VOWELS must be pronounced as in Italian. Of the consonants r is always hard. ђ is like the sound *dy* in the colloquial *how d'ye do*, or the French *di* in *dieu*; ж is the French *j* in *jour*; љ is like the Italian *gl* in *figlio*; њ is like *gn* in *magnifique* (French); ћ is a very difficult sound and can only be learnt from a native. It is something between the sound of *ch* in *church* and *ts*. У is the French *ou* or English *oo*; x is the German guttural as in *acht*, *machen*; ч is *ch* as in *church*; џ corresponds to the English *j* and only occurs in foreign words, especially those which Serbian has borrowed from Turkish; the letter p is frequently used as a vowel, as прст, *a finger*, pronounced *purst*;

this is written in Croatian *pèrst.*—The sound is admirably described by WHITNEY, as quoted in MIKLOSICH, *Vergleichende Grammatik.* Vol. II p. XIV: 'If I may judge from experiments made in my own mouth, the bringing of the *r* Sanskrit far enough forward in the mouth to be trilled would render very natural, and almost unavoidable the slipping in before and after it, of a fragment of the neutral vowel, our *u* in *but....* Of this character it can hardly be doubted, would be what elements the sound contained which were not *r.*'

THE ACCENT. This can in reality only be learnt from a native and all that can be done here is to give a few general rules. The accents are five in number; some however omit the fifth.

The first mark (˝) expresses a short sharp accent, as ко̏ло, *a dance.*—The second mark (`) stands on a short accented syllable;—*e. g.* во̀да, *the water;* вра̀на, *the cow;* ву̀на, *the wool;* зѐмља, *the earth.*—The third mark (´) stands on syllables where the accent is prolonged;—*e. g.* гра́на, *the bough;* о́вца, *the sheep;* се́ка, *the sister.*—The fourth mark (¯) is placed over syllables, where they are to be pronounced at length, and very full;—*e. g.* гла̄д, *hunger;* те̄ло, *the body;* сӯнце, *the sun.*—The fifth mark (ˆ) stands upon syllables, where the accent is much more protracted than in the two preceding instances, as свију̂ наро̂да, *of all peoples.*([1]) The short (`) and long (´) accents never come on the last syllable of a word nor

---

([1]) The Serbian accent changes from one syllable to another in the same word like the Russian and is illustrated by the work on the latter by Prof. JAMES GROTE; the subject has also been specially treated by LESKIEN and NEMANIĆ.

on any monosyllable. Monosyllables only take the following accents: (̏) or (̂) as pȁд, *work*; свêт, *the world*.

The CONSONANTS may be divided as follow:
Labials: б, в, м, п, ф;
Dentals: д, т;
Liquids: л, н, р;
Gutturals: г, к, х;
Sibilants: з, ц, с.
Palatals ħ, ж, ч, ш; semivowel j.

м may also be considered as a labial nasal and н as a dental nasal. This must be borne in mind, if we wish to understand some of the phonetic changes.

The following are the chief modifications which sounds undergo (¹):

1. Vowels which contract in the middle of a word
и-и into и: при-идем = придем, *I come*;
о-о into о: гро-отом = гротом, *with a burst of laughter*.

When for the sake of greater clearness the syllables ought to be kept distinct a disjunctive consonant is added either j, в, д or н, as чу-ем becomes чујем, *I hear*; пи-ем, пијем, *I drink*; да-ати, давати, *to give*; обу-ен, обувен, *with shoes on*; знаем, знадем, *I know*; у-ићи, уићи, *to enter*.

Words that are compounded however do not undergo any contraction, as неук, *ignorant*; црноок, *black-eyed*.

The double vowel *je*, in old times written ѣ (²), in contact with another vowel or with *j* is sometimes changed into и in the middle and at the end of a word,

---

(¹) For some of these remarks I am indebted to Parčic (p. 8).
(²) By those now very few, who do not employ the orthography of VUK. Thus it is found in the Цвѣтникъ Србске Словесности of SUBBOTIĆ (Vienna 1853).

thus: cjeo, сио, *seated*; дjeo, дио, *placed*; see remarks on dialects, page 8.

The law of assimilation causes certain vowels to accompany certain consonants; thus o after .ъ becomes e, as краљем.

2. The conjunction of vowels at the end of a word is avoided *a*) by means of a contraction;—*e. g.* госпа for госпоја, *mistress*;—*b*) by the insertion of the consonant j, as дају, *they give*; пију, *they drink*.

In the ending of nouns, adjectives and participles in a-o, e-o, и-o, y-o, the hiatus is preserved, as it really represents a suppressed л, as ишао, *he went*; пепео, *ashes*; чинио, *he did*; труо, *corrupted*;—to which may also be added орао, *eagle*.

3. Juxtaposition of consonants in the middle of a word.—

a) с, з before soft consonants become soft or palatal: *e. g.* пасче, пашче, *dog*; ту-с-тји, туштји, *fatter*; грозде, грожђе, *grapes*; пазња, пажња, *attention*.

b) ч before т and с becomes ш;—*e. g.* что, што, *what*; чтовати, штовати, *to venerate*; сучанце, сунашце, *the sun*.

c) The consonants д, т, з before т, л are changed into с;—*e. g.* кла-д-ти, класти, *to place;* пле-т-ти, плести, *to knit*; гудле, гусле, *a musical instrument*; ма-з-ло, масло, *butter*.

d) If a guttural precedes ти, the termination of the infinitive, it becomes ћ;—ректи, рећи, *to speak*; стригти, стрићи, *to shear*.

Certain consonants are omitted.

a) The dentals д, т and the labials б, п, в before л, н;—*e. g.* капнути, канути, *to trickle*; гибнути, гинути, *to perish*.

b) The consonant с in the suffixes ск, ств after the palatals;—*e. g.* јунач-с-ки, јуначки, *heroic*; сиромаш-с-ство, сиромаштво, *poverty.*

c) The consonant в in words compounded with об; *e. g.* об-влак = облак, *cloud*; об-власт = област, *power.*

d) The consonant ј after the palatals and р; —*e. g.* дуж-ј-и, дужи, *longer.*

In many instances the letter а is inserted, as стак-лце, becomes стакалце, *little glass*, a diminutive of стакло; sometimes it is у, as предусрести, *to meet.*

Between the labials and the dental т the letter с is added to the infinitive of verbs, as дуб-с-ти, *to dig*, црп-с-ти, *to take*; жив-с-ти, *to live.*

4. Consonants in juxta-position with vowels:

a) Gutturals and sibilants, when the suffix is added, are changed into the corresponding palatals before the suffixes ај, ан, ар, бина, ешина, ев, ић, ица, њи, ски, ство, урина;—*e. g.* пук, *people*, пучки, *popular*; клобук, *hat*, клобучар, *hatter*; корак, *step*, корачај; ђак, *student*, ђачић; јунак, *hero*, јуначина, *great hero*; књига, *book* књижурина, *great book*; отац, *father*, очев, *paternal*; данас, *to-day*, данашњи, *belonging to to-day.*

b) The gutturals and sibilants before е in the inflexions of verbs and masculine nouns become palatals; *e. g.* дихати, *to breathe*, дишем, *I breathe*; дизати, *to raise*, дижем, *I raise*; кнез, *prince*, voc. кнеже; Бог, *god*, voc. Боже.

c) Gutturals in the inflexions of nouns and verbs become sibilants before и;—*e. g.* пук, *people*, пуци (plural); рука, *hand*, руци (dativ); дух, *breath*, дуси (plural); тући (тук-ти), *to beat*; туци (imp.).

The same law holds good in the change of verbs from one aspect to another;—*e. g.* ницѣи (ник-ти), ницати, *to bud*; дигнути, дизати, *to rise*.

5. SOFTENING OF CONSONANTS. Dentals become soft by taking a j, thus дj becomes ђ and тj ћ. So also сj becomes ш, зj, ж and цj ч, and пj and лj become њ and љ. The importance of these rules must be borne in mind when we are forming the irregular comparatives mentioned on page 22.

The Serbian is a much softer language than any of its Slavonic sisters. It has a tendency to elide harsh consonants, sometimes for example at the beginning, as тић, *bird*, which compare with Russian птичка, леб with хлѣбъ, *bread*, so also рапити with храпити and рт with хрт. The liquid л is vocalised, as пун, *full*, Russian полній; пук, *regiment*, Russian полкъ; жут, *yellow*, Russian жёлтый. The tendency to avoid two consonants together has already been noticed, thus леопарад, *leopard*, and others.

It would be impossible in a little work like the present to give anything like an adequate account of the dialects of the Serbian language. As its literature has been so little developed, the student must not be surprised at finding different systems of orthography in vogue. Besides the difference in the use of the interrogative pronoun, which will be mentioned in a subsequent page, the various equivalents used of the Old Slavonic ѣ (*je*) have formed a principle of division into the three following dialects. We will take as tests the words млѣко, *milk*, and вѣра, *faith*, and for greater clearness will make use of the Latin alphabet:

a) Among the Slavonians (in the restricted sense of the inhabitants of that Austrian province), the Dalmatians and the inhabitants of the Adriatic sea-board, *mliko, vira*; this is the Western dialect.

b) In Syrmia, the Banat, the Batchka and Serbia about the Save and Drave, *mleko, vera*;—this is the dialect in which the popular poet RADIČEVIĆ wrote; the Eastern dialect

c) In Bosnia, Herzegovina, Montenegro (Tsrnagora) and in the Southern parts of the kingdom of Serbia in long syllables it is *ije* and in short *je*;—*e.g. mlijeko, vjera*; the Southern dialect.

The Croatian dialect has in many points especially bearing upon phonology become differentiated from the Serb and MIKLOSICH has even gone so far, but it seems to us erroneously, as to consider them different languages!(¹)

The question formed the subject of a valuable article by DANIČIĆ:—Разлике између језика србскога и хрватскога, in the ninth volume of the Гласник, Belgrade, 1857. On the whole, it may be said with truth that these differences between the Serbian and Croatian dialects lie more in the phonetics than in grammatical forms. One of the most noteworthy points of variation in the latter respect is that the Serbs and Dalmatians of the coast use the dual for the plural in the dative, instrumental and locative plural. It will be observed

---

(¹) Vergleichende Grammatik, 1ˢᵗ Vol. p. 392.—But in the first edition of this work he said:—'Die geringen Verschiedenheiten des chorvatischen und serbischen haben mich bestimmt, sie unter einem zu behandeln'.—But we have no space to discuss the question further.

that Serbian and Croatian are treated as the same languages in the two important works of DANIČIĆ:— Облици српскога или хрватскога језика, Agram 1874, and Историја облика српскога или хрватскога језика до свршетка XVII вијека, Belgrade 1876. More Turkish words appear to have crept into Serbian as would naturally result from the geographical position of the country, but these will probably, as the Serbs advance in civilization, be ejected. Before leaving this subject I may add that an excellent treatise on the Ragusan dialect has been published by P. BUDMANI, author of a good Serbo-Croatian Grammar.

PART II:—THE DOCTRINE OF FORMS.

The parts of speech are the same in Serbian as in other languages, with the exception of the article.([1])

The noun has three numbers: the singular, the dual (preserved in a few forms) and the plural, and three genders: masculine, feminine and neuter. There are seven cases: the nominative, genitive, dative, accusative, vocative, locative and instrumental. The only one of these which seems to demand any explanation is the locative, which in some Slavonic languages is called the *prepositional* because it must always be accompanied by a preposition. I have placed the instrumental before the locative in this grammar, for the reasons given at the beginning of my preface.

([1]) It is included in the definite form of the adjective. See page 19.

The Gender of Substantives.

The gender of substantives is partly ascertained by their signification and partly by their termination.—

a. *The signification.*

The names of persons and animals and generally all living beings, whatever be the termination of the substantive are:

1. Masculine, if they denote beings of the male sex, as Бранко, *a proper name*; брат, *brother*; војно, *husband*.

Some contemptuous appellations, however, even when applied to men are of the feminine gender,([1]) as пијаница, *a great drunkard*, скиталица, *a vagabond*. Perhaps similarity of termination may have something to do with this, the feminine ending, as we shall see directly, being frequently in a.

2. Feminine; *a*) all substantives relating to beings of the female sex, as мати, *mother*; сестра, *sister*.— *b*) Collective names of human beings and animals, as браћа, *the brothers*; чељад, *the family*.

b. *The termination.*

Here we can only lay down a few general rules for more minute details the reader must be referred to the dictionaries.

1. Most of the nouns which end in a consonant, or the euphonic о (put for л), are masculine, as роб, *slave*,

---

([1]) This is a characteristic of the Slavonic languages generally, as Miklosich has shewn.

some however which end in ст are feminine, as well as those in -ав and -оћ, as кост, *a bone*; страст, *passion*; љубав, *love*; ноћ, *night*, &c.—Corresponding nouns in Russian end in ь.

2. Most of the nouns which end in a are feminine. Доба, *period*, is neuter, and some nouns are both masculine and feminine, as рат, *war*; вечер, *evening*, &c.

3. The names of all inanimate things ending in е or о are neuter, provided the о be not put euphonically for л as previously explained, as име, *name*; тане, *ball*; поље, *field*; вино, *wine*.

DECLENSION.

I shall divide the Serbian nouns into six declensions according to the plan laid down by MIKLOSICH in his Comparative Grammar, following the analogy of the other Slavonic languages.([1])

I. ъ (a)-STEMS.

The termination is ъ in the Old Slavonic and Russian. This letter however is no longer used according to the modern Serbian spelling.

([1]) A somewhat different arrangement is adopted by DANIČIĆ in his Облици Српскога Језика (Forms of the Serbian Language). Belgrade 1883; but I do not see any reason for altering the system of MIKLOSICH.

DECLENSION.

роб, *a slave.*

	Singular.	*Plural.*
Nom.	роб	роби
Voc.	робе	роби
Acc.	роба	робе
Gen.	роба	роба, роб
Dat.	робу	робима(¹), робом
Instr.	робом	робима, роби
Loc.	робу	робима, робих

In all monosyllabic words and in many two syllabled the syllable ов in the case of stems ending in a hard consonant, and ев in the case of those ending in a soft is added between the stem and the suffix in all cases of the plural. Thus, робови, робова, робовима, &c. In many nouns where a occurs before the final consonant, it is omitted in all cases except the gen. plural as отац, отца, and substantives, which end in с, г, х and з change these consonants in the vocative into the corresponding palatals, as Бог, *God*, Боже.

коњ, *a horse.*

	Singular.	*Plural.*
Nom.	коњ	коњи
Voc.	коњу	коњи
Acc.	коња	коње
Gen.	коња	коња, коњ
Dat.	коњу	коњима, коњем
Instr.	коњем	коњима, коњи
Loc.	коњу	коњима, коњих

In this declension if the noun implies an animate thing the genitive and accusative singular will be identical; if inanimate the noun and accusative singular.

(¹) Those in има and ама were originally dual forms.

II. O-STEMS.

село, *a village.*

	Singular.	*Plural.*
Nom.	село	села
Acc.	село	села
Gen.	села	села, сел
Dat.	селу	селима, селом
Instr.	селом	селима, сели
Loc.	селу	селима, селих

поље, *a field.*(¹)

	Singular.	*Plural.*
Nom.	поље	поља
Acc.	поље	поља
Gen.	поља	поља, пољ
Dat.	пољу	пољима, пољем
Instr.	пољем	пољима, пољи
Loc.	пољу	пољима, пољих

III. a-STEMS.

риба, *a fish.*

	Singular.	*Plural.*
Nom.	риба	рибе
Voc.	рибо	рибе
Acc.	рибу	рибе
Gen.	рибе	риба, риб
Dat.	риби	рибама, рибам
Instr.	рибом	рибама, рибами
Loc.	риби	рибама, рибах

(¹) The insertion of **поље** among the o-stems is explained by the stem being **пољо**. The final-o preceded by a consonant, which has been modified by j, becomes e.

воља, *will.*

	Singular.	*Plural.*
Nom.	воља	воље
Voc.	вољо	воље
Acc.	вољу	воље
Gen.	воље	воља, вољ
Dat.	вољи	вољама, вољам
Instr.	вољом	вољама, вољами
Loc.	вољи	вољама, вољах

IV. ъ (*u*)-STEMS.

The old ъ (*u*)-stems follow the declension of the ъ (*a*)-stems. The Croatian still employs the sing. voc. sinu, Old Slav. сыну. We have traces of the declension of the ъ (*u*)-stems in the dat. and voc. sing. and in the syllable ов of the ъ (*a*)-stems.

V. ь-STEMS.

1. *masculine.*

Of the Old Slavonic masculine declension in ь (*ĭ*) there are but scanty remains.

2. *feminine.*

кост, *a bone.*

	Singular.	*Plural.*
Nom.	кост	кости
Voc.	кости	кости
Acc.	кост	кости
Gen.	кости	кости, jу([1])
Dat.	кости	костима, костим
Instr.	кошћу	костима, костми
Loc.	кости	костима, костих

([1]) The dual form костију is occasionally found.

VI. CONSONANTAL STEMS.

a) в-stems.

Of these there are a few traces.

b) н-stems.

1. *masculine.*

Among these дан, *day*, may be mentioned, which is very irregular. The chief forms are as follow:

	Singular.	Plural.
Nom.	дан	дани, дни
Voc.	дане	дани
Acc.	дан	дане, дни
Gen.	дана, дне, дни	дана, днева
Dat.	дану, дне	данима
Instr.	даном, дању	данима
Loc.	дану, дне	данима

2. *neuter.*

име, *a name.*

	Singular.	Plural.
Nom.	име	имена
Acc.	име	имена
Gen.	имена	имена, имен
Dat.	имену	именима, имен
Instr.	именом	именима, имени
Loc.	имену	именима, имених

c) с-stems.

тијело, *the body.*

	Singular.	Plural.
Nom.	тијело	тјелеса
Acc.	тијело	тјелеса
Gen.	тијела	тјелеса, тилес
Dat.	тијелу	тјелесима, тилесом
Instr.	тијелом	тјелесима, тилеси
Loc.	тијелу	тјелесима, тилесих

In this way are also declined небо, *heaven*, and чудо, *a wonder*; око, *an eye*, and ухо, *an ear*, use as plural the old dual:—очи, уши. очију, ушију, очима, ушима.

d) т-stems.

тане, *a ball (of a musket)*.

	Singular.	Plural.
Nom.	тане	танета
Acc.	тане	танета
Gen.	танета	танета, танет
Dat.	танету	танетима, танетом
Instr.	танетом	танетима, танети
Loc.	танету	танетима, танетих

Irregular nouns belonging to this declension are псето, *dog*, gen. псета and псетета and дрво a tree which makes plur. дрвета, *clubs*, and дрва, *logs of wood*.

e) p-stems.

мати, *a mother*.

	Singular.	Plural.
Nom.	мати	матере
Acc.	матер	матере
Gen.	матере	матера, матер
Dat.	матери	матерама, матерам
Instr.	матером	матерама, матерами
Loc.	матери	матерама, матерах

ћи, *a daughter*, has in the singular accusative ћер, but in other respects follows the paradigm кост. As this noun is in such common use it is added.

в

	Singular.	Plural.
Nom.	кћи (sometimes but incorrectly кћер)	кћери
Acc.	кћер	кћери
Gen.	кћери	кћери
Dat.	кћери	кћерима, кћерим
Instr.	кћери	кћерима, кћермн
Loc.	кћери	кћерих

As previously observed, according to the rule of Slavonic languages in the case of animate things the genitive and accusative are the same, in the singular number and masculine gender; in the case of inanimate things the nominative and accusative.

It would occupy too much space in this grammar to give a list of nouns defective in number which can easily be learned from the dictionary; thus *e. g.* ножице, *scissors*, and топлице, *hot baths*, are only used in the plural. Доба, *a period*, is of the neuter gender and indeclinable.

A few more irregular nouns may be specified, thus брат pl. браћа, which becomes a collective feminine noun and is declined like риба; човјек, *man*, has for pl. људи (cf. Russian). Many names of inanimate things become collective neuters in the plural, thus цвиет, *a flower*; цвиеће, *a bunch of flowers*; лист, *a leaf*; лишће, *a bunch of leaves*. This is a striking peculiarity of the language and should be noted. Груди and прси, *breast*, have a dual form, one of the remains of the old language and the same applies to плећи, *shoulders*; thus gen. грудију, прсију, плећију, dat. грудима, прсима, плећима.

Of the various terminations of nouns the following are worthy of specification:

a) The male agent is expressed by the termination -ац, as ловац, *hunter*; писац, *writer*; sometimes -ач, as ковач, *blacksmith*; feminine -ица, as ковачица; -ар, as књижар, *bookseller*, and -ик, as милосник, *a lover*.

b) -анин to express the place or country from which one comes, as Бечанин, *a native of Vienna*. This is sometimes expressed by the termination -лија, as Цариградлија, *a native of Constantinople*.

c) -ство the function, as учитељство, *the function of being teacher*.

d) -ска, denoting country, as Инглеска, *England*.

e) -ање andење to express an action or its effects, as читање, *the act of reading*, or -ба, as берба, *the gathering of grapes*.

f) -иште, place, as позориште, *theatre*.

g) Diminutives, -ић, as ножић, *a little knife*; -ца, as ноћца, *little night*; -ка, as сека, *little sister*.(¹)

h) -ад, denotes collectives, as прасад, *a herd of swine*; штенад, *a litter of puppies*.

ADJECTIVES.

In Serb the adjective has two forms, the indefinite and the definite;—*e. g.* indef. млад човјек, *a young man*; млади човјек, *the young man*. In reality as has been shewn by Miklosich and other scholars the -и of the termination is the definite article, and this is why (in appearance) an article is wanting in the Slavonic languages.

But all adjectives do not possess both indefinite and definite forms:—1) possessive adjectives in ов, ев and ин can only have the indefinite form. 2) All the other possessive adjectives, the ordinal numbers as well as

---

(¹) Also села, селе, thus а да јоште ти ме видиш, селе, *and that thou mayst still see me, sister* — M. Ban.

в*

the following, десни, *on the right hand*; лиеви, *on the left hand*; цигли, *unique*; обьи, *general*; остали, *remaining*; мали, *little*; вељи, *great*; дивљи, *savage*, and some others have only the definite form.

Indefinite Adjective.

млад, *young*.

Singular.

	Masculine.	Feminine.	Neuter.
Nom.	млад	млада	младо
Acc.	млада (animate) / млад (inanimate)	младу	младо
Gen.	млада	младе	млада
Dat.	младу	младој	младу
Instr.	младим	младом	младим
Loc.	младу	младој	младу

Plural.

	Masculine.	Feminine.	Neuter.
Nom.	млади	младе	млада
Acc.	младе	младе	млада
Gen.		младих	
Dat.	младима	младим	*for all genders*
Instr.	младима	младими	
Loc.	младима	младих	

Definite Adjective.

Singular.

	Masculine.	Feminine.	Neuter.
Nom.	млади	млада	младо
Acc.	младога (animate) / млади (inanimate)	младу	младо
Gen.	младога	младе	младога
Dat.	младому	младој	младому
Instr.	младим	младом	младим
Loc.	младом	младој	младом

ADJECTIVES.

Plural.

	Masculine.	Feminine.	Neuter.
Nom.	млади	младе	млада
Acc.	младе	младе	млада
Gen.		младих	
Dat.	младима	младим	}
Instr.	младима	младими	} for all genders
Loc.	младима	младих	}

It will be observed that the accusative masculine, as in substantives, has two forms one for animate, the other for inanimate things.

In the genitive and dative singulars of the masculine and neuter the final vowel is sometimes suppressed, thus ог, ом, ем.

The example млад illustrates the declension of an adjective, which terminates in a hard consonant; in the case of one ending in a soft consonant;—*e. g.* врућ, *warm*, the only differences in the indefinite form are that the neuter nom. and acc. ends in e, as врућe, and in the definite the gen. masc. is врућега and the dative врућему, the locative врућем; the neuter nom. and acc. are врућe, gen. and dat. same as the masc. The plural of the adjective in the definite form is the same whether with a hard or soft termination.

The irregular adjective вас or сав is here added on account of its frequent use.

Singular.

	Masculine.	Feminine.	Neuter.
Nom.	вас, сав	сва	све
Acc.	вас, сав, свега (animate)	сву	све
Gen.	свега	све	свега
Dat.	свему	свој	свему
Instr.	свим	свом	свим
Loc.	свем	свој	свем

Plural.

	Masculine.	Feminine.	Neuter.
Nom.	сви	све	сва
Acc.	све	све	сва
Gen.		свих	
Dat.	свима	свим	
Instr.	свима	свими	} for all genders
Loc.	свима	свих	

DEGREES OF COMPARISON.

The comparative degree is ordinarily expressed by adding to the stems the terminationsији for the masculine, ија for the feminine and ије for the neuter, thus богат, *rich,* comp. богатији, -ија, -ије. Many adjectives, however, of two syllables which end in ак, ек and ок reject thus final syllable and add ји, ја, је to the stem;—*e. g.* низак, *low,* comp. нижи; далек, *afar off,* comparative даљи; висок, *high,* comp. виши; широк, *broad,* comp. шири.(¹)

The following four comparatives which are in frequent use are altogether irregular.

добар, *good*; comp. бољи
зао, *bad*; comp. гори
мали, *little*; comp. мањи
велик, *great*; comp. већи

The superlative is expressed by the addition of the syllable нај- to the comparative;—*e. g.* највећи, *the greatest*; најбољи, *the best.*

(¹) This may no doubt be explained by the fact that к and its accompanying vowels are suffixes. Cf. Old Slavonic велій, Russ. великій, *great*; диво Russ. and Chekh divoký. The final consonant of the stem is modified by the phonetic laws previously stated.

THE NUMERALS.

1. Cardinal.

један, -дна, -дно	1	двадесет и један	21
два, двие, два	2	тридесет	30
три	3	четрдесет	40
четири	4	педесет	50
пет	5	шездесет or шесет	60
шест	6	седамдесет	70
седам	7	осамдесет	80
осам	8	деведесет	90
девет	9	сто	100
десет	10	сто и један	101
једанаест	11	сто и двадесет	120
дванаест	12	двиеста, двие стотине	200
тринаест	13	триста, три стотине	300
четрнаест	14	четири стотине	400
двадесет	20	тисућа, хиљада	1000

2. Ordinals.

први	first
други	second
трећи (трети)	third
четврти	fourth
пети	fifth

And so on, each being declined as a definite adjective, but as these numerals may easily be found in a dictionary, I have not thought it necessary to lose space by recapitulating them here.

The first cardinal number један is declined like are indefinite adjective the three next are declined with feminine substantives, and agree with the noun, with masculine and neuter nouns they are treated as indeclinable and the noun to which they refer is in the genitive singular, but after пет, *five*, all the nouns are in the genitive plural. This (apparent) genitive singular used only in the case of masculine and neuter nouns is considered by Miklosich to be in reality a corrupt form of the dual, as we find in Russian.

The declension of два, три and четири is as follows:

N. A.	двие(¹)	три	четири
G. L.	двију	трију	четирију
D.	двјема	трима	четирима
I.	двјема	трими	четирими

Dates are indicated in Serb in the following way. For the days of the month we use ordinals;—*e. g.* први, други, трећи (дан being understood) мјесеца, *the first, second, third of the month*; for the manner of expressing the year see page 64. When there are several numerals together, the last of them governs the noun, as двадесет и два човјека, *twenty-two men*. Оба and обадва, *both*, are declined like два only in the feminine. Collective numerals in Serbian end in -ица, as петерица, *a party of five*.

Serbian has an interesting parallel to the expression familiar to classical scholars τέταρτος αὐτός *i. e.* with three others, the idea is exactly expressed by самочетврт.

PRONOUNS.

The pronouns are divided into personal, demonstrative, interrogative, relative and indefinite. Under the personal are also included possessive pronouns.

(¹) The masculine and neuter forms of два are no longer declined.

PRONOUNS.

PERSONAL PRONOUNS.

First person.

	Singular.	Plural.
Nom.	ја	ми
Acc.	мене, ме	нас
Gen.	мене, ме	нас
Dat.	мени, ми	нама нам
Instr.	мном (меном)	нама нами
Loc.	мени	нама нас

Second person.

	Singular.	Plural.
Nom.	ти	ви
Acc.	тебе, те	вас
Gen.	тебе, те	вас
Dat.	теби, ти	вама вам
Voc.	ти	ви
Instr.	тобом	вама вами
Loc.	теби	вама вас

Third person.

Singular.

	Masculine.	Feminine.	Neuter.
Nom.	он	она	оно
Acc.	њега, га	њу, ју	њега, га
Gen.	њега, га	ње, је	њега, га
Dat.	њему, му	њој, јој	њему, му
Instr.	њим	њом	њим
Loc.	њем	њој	њем

Plural.

	Masculine.	Feminine.	Neuter.	
Nom.	они	оне	она	
Acc.		ње, је, њих		
Gen.		њих, јих, их		for all genders
Dat.	њима	њим, јим		
Instr.	њима	њими		
Loc.	њима	њих		

THE REFLEXIVE PRONOUN.

This pronoun may be employed with all persons and both numbers.

Acc.	себе, се
Gen.	себе, се
Dat.	себи, си
Instr.	себи
Loc.	собом

The shorter forms are more often employed, and are like enclitics. In common with the other Slavonic languages the longer forms of the prepositions are used, when emphasis is required. After prepositions the accusative of the pronoun он is shortened into њ. Thus И у један пут нападе нањ мрак и тама—*and immediately there fell upon him mist and darkness.* Acts XIII, 11.

The possessive pronouns are inflected as follows:

мој, *mine.*

Singular.

	Masculine.	Feminine.	Neuter.
Nom.	мој	моја	моје
Acc.	мојега, мога	моју	моје
Gen.	мојега, мога	моје	мојега, мога
Dat.	мојему, мому	мојој	мојему, мому
Voc.	мој	моја	моје
Instr.	мојим	мојом	мојим
Loc.	мојем, мом	мојој	мојем, мом

Plural.

	Masculine.	Feminine.	Neuter.
Nom.	моји	моје	моја
Acc.	моје	моје	моја
Gen.		мојих	for all genders
Dat.	мојима	мојим	for all genders
Voc.	моје	моје	моја
Instr.	мојима	мојими	for all genders
Loc.	мојима	мојих (-нех)	for all genders

наш, *our.*

Singular.

	Masculine.	Feminine.	Neuter.
Nom.	наш	наша	наше
Acc.	нашега	нашу	наше
Gen.	нашега	наше	нашега
Dat.	нашему	нашој	нашему
Voc.	наш	наша	наше
Instr.	нашим	нашом	нашим
Loc.	нашем	нашој	нашем

Plural.

	Masculine.	Feminine.	Neuter.
Nom.	наши	наше	наша
Acc.	наше	наше	наша
Gen.		наших } for all genders	
Dat.	нашима	нашим	
Voc.	наше	наше	наша
Instr.	нашима	нашими } for all genders	
Loc.	нашима	наших	

твој, *thy*, and свој, the reflexive, are declined like мој. ваш, *your*, is declined like наш.

The other possessive pronouns follow the inflexions of the adjectives of the indefinite form, such are његов, *belonging to him* or *it*, њезин, *belonging to her*, њихов *belonging to them*; моја, твоја and моје, твоје are sometimes, especially in poetry, contracted into ма, тва, ме, тве; свој is used indiscriminately for all persons and numbers, as Ја љубим своју домовину, *I love my country.*

Demonstrative Pronouns.

These are five in number:
1) овај, ова, ово, *this.*
2) тај, та, то, *this* or *that.*

3) онај, она, оно, *that*.
4) исти, иста, исто, *the same*.
5) сам, сама, само, *alone, only one*.

These pronouns are declined in the following manner:

Singular.

	Masculine.	Feminine.	Neuter.
Nom.	овај	ова	ово
Acc.	овај, овога (animate)	ову	ово
Gen.	овога	ове	овога
Dat.	овому	овој	овому
Instr.	овим	овом	овим
Loc.	овом	овој	овом

Plural.

	Masculine.	Feminine.	Neuter.
Nom.	ови	ове	ова
Acc.	ове	ове	ова
Gen.		ових	
Dat.		овим	
Instr.		овими	
Loc.		ових	

тај, *this* or *that*, has something of the sense of the Latin *ille* and is not very easily translated in our language.

Singular.

	Masculine.	Feminine.	Neuter.
Nom.	тај	та	то
Acc.	тај, тог	ту	то
Gen.	тога	те	тога
Dat.	тому	тој	тому
Instr.	тијем, тим	том	тијем, тим
Loc.	том	тој	том

PRONOUNS.

Plural.

	Masculine.	Feminine.	Neuter.
Nom.	ти	те	та
Acc.	те	те	та
Gen.		тијех, тих	
Dat.	тијема	тим	
Instr.	тијема	тими	} for all genders
Loc.	тијема	тих	

I have added the duals throughout the pronouns as they are used by the Serbs in contradistinction to the Croats.

INTERROGATIVE AND RELATIVE PRONOUNS.

	тко, *who.*	што, *what.*
Nom.	тко, ко	што, шта
Acc.	кога	што (шта)
Gen.	кога	чеса, чега (шта)
Dat.	кому	чему
Instr.	ким, кнем	чим (чнем)
Loc.	ком	чем

They have no plural.

We now have the interrogative and relative pronoun који, which is declined like an adjective.

Singular.

	Masculine.	Feminine.	Neuter.
Nom.	који (ки) (¹)	која (ка)	које (ко)
Acc.	којега (кога)	које (ке)	којега (кога)
Gen.	којему (кому)	којој (кој)	којему (кому)
Dat.	којн, којега (кога)	којy (ку)	које (ко)
Instr.	којим (ким)	којом (ком)	којим (ким)
Loc.	којем (ком)	којој (кој)	којем (ком)

(¹) Also sometimes written кој.

Plural.

	Masculine.	Feminine.	Neuter.
Nom.	који (ки)	које (ке)	која (ка)
Acc.	које (ке)	које (ке)	која (ка)
Gen.		којих (ких)	
Dat.	којима	којим (ким)	for all genders
Instr.	којима	којими (кими)	
Loc.	којима	којих (ких)	

In the same way is declined чиј, *belonging to whom*. Converted with these pronouns are the adjectival forms чигов, *belonging to whom*; колик, *how great*; каков and какав, *of what sort*.

шта is often used for што in the colloquial language, and is indeed several times introduced by VUK in his translation of the New Testament. Instead of this the Dalmatians use ча (*ča*) and the Slovenes kaj; hence the distinction between the štokavci, the čakavci and the kajkavci, with which FEUVRIER well compares the difference between the *langue d'oil* and the *langue d'oc*.

INDEFINITE PRONOUNS.

Such are њетко, *a certain person*, њешто a certain thing, сватко, *each*, and others declined like тко, and their corresponding adjectives, њекоји, штокоји, сваки &c. which can easily be learned from the dictionaries, and must be omitted here for want of space.

THE VERB.

The Serbian verbs may be divided as follow:

1) Active and passive, transitive, neuter and reflexive, considered with regard to their signification.

2) Simple and compound, primitive and derived with regard to their form.

3) Perfective and imperfective from the point of view of the duration of the action. It is with the last of these three divisions which we have more particularly to do, verbs of this class are said to be arranged according to their aspects, a feature peculiar to the Slavonic languages. In a short grammar like the present it will only be possible to give the leading principles of this classification. For more minute details the reader must use a good Serbian dictionary, and above all, must make himself familiar with the great comparative Grammar of MIKLOSICH.(¹)

The perfective aspect denotes either that the action has been quite completed, or that it will definitely cease. This aspect has no present tense, but a present form with a future signification, just as we say in English: 'I go to-morrow morning'. Many of the verbs belonging to this aspect are compounded with prepositions, as изпити, *to drink up.*

The perfective verbs are again subdivided either: *a*) as they denote completion without regard to the duration of the action;—*e. g.* купити, *to buy*, in one or more acts (unconditional perfective verbs) or *b*) with reference to the duration of the action (conditional perfective verbs). In the last circumstance the action may be either α) one the beginning and end of which are simultaneous, as стријељати, *to shoot*, the action being done rapidly, once for all as it were: these verbs are called by MIKLOSICH momentaneous, and correspond to the perfect aspect of unity of the Russian grammarians or

---

(¹) Vergleichende Grammatik der Slavischen Sprachen. Vienna 1883. 4th Vol., p. 274.

β) the action may not have a simultaneous beginning and end and this class is further subdivided into 1) where the action the completion of which is predicated, is a continuous one or 2) repeated at various times. The first of these MIKLOSICH calls durative perfective, the second iterative perfective.

The imperfective verbs express an action that is not completed but this may be conceived either *a*) as merely continuing or *b*) repeated at various times. The verbs of the first class are called durative, the verbs of the second class, iterative, and of these last there are two forms, but into further minutiae it is impossible to enter here. .Enough has been given to shew the riches of the Slavonic verbal system.

Each aspect is regularly conjugated according to its own moods and tenses.

a) The imperfective aspect has all the moods and tenses.

b) The perfective wants the present and imperfect tenses.

c) The iterative has no present tense, and is also deficient in the imperative mood.

The various aspects are arranged under the six conjugations, according to the system, which follows immediately in the grammar.([1]) Thus one aspect of a verb will belong to one conjugation and another aspect to another. The knowledge of these aspects can only be gained by the use of a good dictionary, as they vary greatly both in termination and prefix, and it is the

---

([1]) For remarks on these involving much minute detail the student must consult MIKLOSICH.

large employment of the prepositions for this latter purpose which makes the study of them so important in the Slavonic languages. A list of the most common of them with their various uses is therefore added.

Besides the aspects of verbs already noticed there are also diminutive verbs, as говоркати, *to speak a little*, скакутати, *to hop about a little*. Similar forms are also to be found in the Upper-Sorbish and Malo-Russian languages. Verbs which have every aspect are rarely found.

The iterative aspect may often be known by the termination -ати or -авати, thus дати, *to give*, давати, *to give often*; спати, *to sleep*, спавати, *to sleep often*. Sometimes the aspect is determined by the accent of which examples can be seen in MIKLOSICH, Vergleichende Grammatik IV, 282.

Compound verbs are those which take a preposition before them. The prefixes which must be learned by consulting a dictionary have no influence upon the conjugation of a verb, for it is a rule that compound verbs follow the conjugation of the simple verb from which they are derived.

A few of the prefixes, however, are here introduced to guide the reader in the changes of the various aspects.

до, which implies carrying the action to the extremity, as дохранити, *to guard to the end*.

на, has somewhat of the same signification, as наиграти се, *to play till one is tired out*.

о, об, sometimes signifies around, as окресати, *to cut the edges round*, and sometimes intensifies the signification. It also helps to form the perfect aspect, as опити, *to get drunk*. Cf. the uses of пјевао and опјевао in the extract at the end of the Grammar.

c

од, ода, gives the idea of separation, as одагнати, *to drive away*.

по sometimes gives to imperfect verbs the signification of perfect, as попити, *to drink to the dregs*.

под expresses underneath, like the Latin *sub*, as подјармити, *to put under the yoke, to subjugate*.

пре implie change, going from one place to another, as пебродити, *to cross a river*.

пред, before, as предброити, *to pay beforehand, to subscribe*.

раз expresses the idea of destruction or diffusion, as разградити, *to demolish*.

с, са, denotes either *a*) union, as саставити, *to join*, or *b*) descent, as с-лазити, *to descend from*.

у, in, either *a*) implies entrance, as улазити, *to enter*, or *b*) gives the tense of completed action, as упалити, *to set on fire*.

уз, up either *a*) has this sense simply, as узићи, *to mount*; *b*) or gives to imperfect verse the sense of perfect, as узплодити, *to fructify*; *c*) it is used to make the future simple conditional of an ordinary verb, as is afterwards shewn on page 56, as ако узхтијем, *if I should wish.* (¹)

за is sometimes used in the sense of beginning, as започети, *to begin*.

The following are the original personal suffixes, which are either present or have disappeared through phonetic decay in the tenses.

(¹) Those who spell phonetically write this з in many cases с, thus усплодити is more usual than узплодити.

	Singular.	Plural.
1.	м	мо
2.	сп	те
3.	т	нт

The т of the 3d pers. singular and plural is lost. The connecting vowel is e or o, as may be seen in the forms of the tenses.

The verbs of the class marked B, where there is no present suffix, such as јад, дад, вêд and јес are considered by MIKLOSICH to be remains of an older stage of the language, when the present was formed without e.

The conjugations of the Serbian verb will be here arranged, according to the system of MIKLOSICH. Before, however, giving the several classes of verbs, it will be as well to give his analysis of the Slavonic verb generally. Each verb has two stems, firstly the infinitive stem and secondly the present stem.

1) THE INFINITIVE STEM.—In this the verbs are divided into two classes, according as they add the verbal suffixes immediately to the root, or add them to the root or a noun or verbal-stem by means of one of the following suffixes: nq ([1]), e, i, a, ua (ova). Putting these two together we may say that verbal stems are divided into six classes:

a) Stems without suffixes;
b) nq-stems;
c) ê-stems;

---

[1] By q is expressed the nasal, which existed in Old-Slavonic, and although now lost, influences the verb and explains the principles of its conjugation.

d) *i*-stems;
e) *a*-stems;
f) *ova*-stems.

The special infinitive stems are:—1) the infinitive, 2) the supine, 3) 1st past participle active, 4) 2nd past participle active, 5) past participle passive, 6) aorist.

2) THE PRESENT STEMS are:—1) the present, 2) imperative, 3) imperfect, 4) present participle active, 5) present participle passive.

According to the present stems the verbs fall into two classes, as the forms of the present are made with the help of the present suffix-*e* or without it.

A.—CONJUGATION WITH THE PRESENT SUFFIX.

First class.

STEMS WITHOUT SUFFIXES.

I. плет, *to braid*.

α) inf. stem плет; inf. плес-ти; past part. active I плетав([1]), плетавши; II плео; past part. passive плетен.

AORIST.

Sg.	1 плет-о-х	Pl.	плет-о-с-мо
	2 плет-е		плет-о-с-те
	3 плет-е		плет-о-ш-е

β) present stem плет-е.

PRESENT.

Sg.	1 плет-е-м	Pl.	плет-е-мо
	2 плет-е-ш		плет-е-те
	3 плет-е		плету

([1]) The indeclinable forms of the participles are sometimes called gerunds.

CONJUGATION WITH THE PRESENT SUFFIX.

IMPERATIVE.

Sg. 1   Pl. плет-п-мо
    2 плет-и   плет-и-те

IMPERFECT

Sg. 1 плет-нја-х   Pl. плет-нја-с-мо
    2 плет-нја-ш-е   плет-нја-с-те
    3 плет-нја-ш-е   плет-нја-х-у
    PART. PRES. ACT. плет-уѣн

II. пас, *to pasture*.

α) inf. stem пас; inf. пас-ти; past part. act. I пасав, пасавши; II пасао; past part. passive пасен.

AORIST.

Sg. 1 пас-о-х   Pl. пас-о-с-мо
    2 пас-е   пас-о-с-те
    3 пас-е   пас-о-ш-е

β) present stem пасе.

PRESENT.

Sg. 1 пас-е-м   Pl. пас-е-мо
    2 пас-е-ш   пас-е-те
    3 пас-е   пас-у

IMPERATIVE.

Sg. 1   Pl. пас-и-мо
    2 пас-и   пас-и-те

IMPERFECT.

Sg. 1 пас-нја-х   Pl. пас-нја-с-мо
    2 пас-нја-ш-е   пас-нја-с-те
    3 пас-нја-ш-е   пас-нја-х-у
    PART. PRES. ACT. пас-уѣн

III. греб, to scratch.

α) inf. stem греб; inf. греб-с-ти; past part. act. I гребав, гребавши; II гребао; past part. passive гребен.

Aorist.

Sg.	1 греб-о-х	Pl. греб-о-с-мо
	2 греб-е	греб-о-с-те
	3 греб-е	греб-о-ш-е

β) present stem греб-е.

Present.

Sg.	1 греб-е-м	Pl. греб-е-мо
	2 греб-е-ш	греб-е-те
	3 греб-е	греб-у

Imperative.

Sg.	1	Pl. греб-и-мо
	2 греб-и	греб-и-те

Imperfect.

Sg.	1 греб-иja-х	Pl. греб-иja-с-мо
	2 греб-иja-ш-е	греб-иja-с-те
	3 греб-иja-ш-е	греб-иja-х-у

Part. Pres. Act. греб-ући.

IV. пек, to bake.

α) inf. stem пек; inf. пећи; past part. act. I пекав, пекавши; II пекао; past. part. passive печен.

Aorist.

Sg.	1 пек-о-х	Pl. пек-о-с-мо
	2 печ-е	пек-о-с-те
	3 печ-е	пек-о-ш-е

β) present stem пек-е.

PRESENT.

Sg. 1 печ-е-м Pl. печ-е-мо
2 печ-е-ш печ-е-те
3 печ-е пек-у

IMPERATIVE.

Sg. 1 Pl. пец-и-мо
2 пеци пец-и-те

IMPERFECT.

Sg. 1 пец-иja-x Pl. пец-иja-с-мо
2 пец-иja-ш-е пец-иja-с-те
3 пец-иja-ш-е пец-иja-x-у

PART. PRES. ACT. пек-ўи

V. кльн(¹), *to curse*.

α) inf. stem кле; inf. кле-ти; past part. act. I клев, кле-в-ши; II кле-о; past part. passive клет.

AORIST.

Sg. 1 клех Pl. кле-с-мо
2 кле кле-с-те
3 кле кле-ш-е

β) present stem кльн-е.

PRESENT.

Sg. 1 кун-е-м Pl. кун-е-мо
2 кун-е-ш кун-е-те
3 кун-е кун-у

IMPERATIVE.

Sg. 1 Pl. кун-и-мо
2 куни кун-и-те

(¹) The ь is used by MIKLOSICH to express the short i (ĭ) between л and н.

IMPERFECT.

Sg. 1 кун-пја-х   Pl. кун-пја-с-мо
    2 кун-њјаш--е   кун-пја-с-те
    3 кун-пја-ш-е   кун-пја-х-у
    PRES. PART. ACT. кун-yћн.

VI. мр, *to die.*

α) inf. stem мр; inf. мр-ње-ти; past part. act. I мр-в, мр-вши; II мро; past part. passive треп.(¹)

AORIST.

Sg. 1 мр-пје-х   Pl. мр-ње-с-мо
    2 мр-пје   мр-пје-с-те
    3 мр-пје   мр-ње-ш-е

β) present stem мре.

PRESENT.

Sg. 1 мр-е-м   Pl. мр-е-мо
    2 мр-е-ш   мр-е-те
    3 мре   мр-у

IMPERATIVE.

Sg. 1   Pl. мр-и-мо
    2 мри   мр-и-те

IMPERFECT.

Sg. 1 (прах)   мрах   Pl. (пр-а-с-мо)   мр-а-с-мо
    2 (пр-а-ш-е) мр-а-ш-е   (пр-а-с-те)   мр-а-с-те
    3 (пр-а-ш-е) мр-а-ш-е   (пр-а-х-у)(²) мр-а-х-у
    PRES. PART. ACT. мр-yћн.

(¹) The past participle passive of the verb мр is wanting and to complete the paradigm in its place is put that of the verb трти. Cf. DANIČIĆ, Облнци Српс. Језика 91.

(²) MIKLOSICH gives this as supplied from the verb прати, *to wash*, a regular form however is given in мр-а-х by DANIČIĆ, Об. С. Ј. 90.

CONJUGATION WITH THE PRESENT SUFFIX.

VII. би, *to beat.*

α) inf. stem би; inf. би-ти; past part. act. I бив, би-вши; II би-о; past part. passive бит.

AORIST.

Sg. 1 би-х   Pl. би-с-мо
    2 би   би-с-те
    3 би   би-ш-е

β) present stem би-j-е.

PRESENT.

Sg. 1 би-j-е-м   Pl. би-j-е-мо
    2 би-j-е-ш   би-j-е-те
    3 би-j-е   би-j-у

IMPERATIVE.

Sg. 1   Pl. би-j-мо
    2 биj   би-j-те

IMPERFECT.

Sg. 1 би-j-а-х   Pl. би-j-а-с-мо
    2 би-j-а-ш-е   би-j-а-с-те
    3 би-j-а-ш-е   би-j-а-ху

PRES. PART. ACT. би-j-ѣи.

Second class.

nq-STEMS (in the Old-Slavonic with a nasalized *a*).

тону, *to sink.*

α) inf. stem тону; inf. тону-ти; past part. act. I тонув, тонувши; II тону-о; past part. passive тегнут.(¹)

(¹) There is no past participle passive to this verb, and to complete the form it is supplied from verbs like затегнути. See Daničić, p. 93. The root is топ, compare потоп, *a flood;* the п has dropped out.

Aorist.

	Sg.		Pl.
1	тону-х		тону-с-мо
2	тону		тону-с-те
3	тону		тону-ш-е

β) present stem тон-е.

Present.

	Sg.		Pl.
1	тон-е-м		тон-е-мо
2	тон-е-ш		тон-е-те
3	тон-е		тон-у

Imperative.

	Sg.		Pl.
1			тон-и-мо
2	тон-и		тон-и-те

Imperfect.

	Sg.		Pl.
1	тон-ja-х		тон-ja-с-мо
2	тон-ja-ш-е		тон-ja-с-те
3	тон-ja-ш-е		тон-ja-х-у

Pres. Part. Act. тон-уħи.

Third class.

ê-Stems.

First group.

умê, *to understand, to know.*

α) inf. stem умje; inf. умje-ти; past part act. I умje-в, умjев-ши; II ум-и-о; past part. passive шти-в-е-н.(¹).

Aorist.

	Sg.		Pl.
1	умje-х		умje-с-мо
2	умje		умje-с-те
3	умje		умje-ш-е

(¹) штивен is borrowed from the verb штити, *to read*, to complete the paradigm.

CONJUGATION WITH THE PRESENT SUFFIX.   43

β) present stem умиј-е.

PRESENT.

Sg. 1 уми-ј-е-м Pl. уми-ј-е-мо
  2 умн-ј-е-ш   уми-ј-е-те
  3 уми-ј-е   уми-ј-у

IMPERATIVE.

Sg. 1   Pl. уми-ј-мо
  2 уми-ј   уми-ј-те

IMPERFECT.

Sg. 1 уми-ја-х Pl. уми-ја-с-мо
  2 уми-ја-ш-е   уми-ја-с-те
  3 уми-ја-ш-е   умн-ја-х-у

PRES. PART. ACT. уми-ј-ућн.

Second group.

горê, *to burn.*

α) inf. stem горје; inf. горје-ти; past part. act. I горјев, горјевши; II горио; past part. passive видје-н.(¹)

AORIST.

Sg. 1 горје-х Pl. горје-с-мо
  2 горје   горје-о-те
  3 горје   горје-ш-е

β) present stem гори-е.

PRESENT.

Sg. 1 гори-м Pl. гори-мо
  2 гори-ш   гори-те
  3 гори   горе

(¹) This has been taken by MIKLOSICH from a corresponding form видјети, *to see*, which is the specimen given by Daničić, Об. Ср. Јез. 98.

Imperative.

Sg. 1   Pl. гори-мо
   2 гори   гори-те

Imperfect.

Sg. 1 гори-ја-х   Pl. гори-ја-с-мо
   2 гори-ја-ш-е   гори-ја-с-те
   3 гори-ја-ш-е   гори-ја-х-у

Pres. Part. Act. горећи.

Fourth class.

i-Stems.

хвали, *to praise.*

α) inf. stem хвали; inf. хвали-ти; past part. act. I хвалив, хвали-вши; II хвали-о; past part. passive хвалј-е-н.

Aorist.

Sg. 1 хвалих   Pl. хвали-с-мо
   2 хвали   хвали-с-те
   3 хвали   хвали-ш-е

β) present stem хвали-е.

Present.

Sg. 1 хвалим   Pl. хвали-мо
   2 хвалиш   хвали-те
   3 хвали   хвале

Imperative.

Sg. 1   Pl. хвали-мо
   2 хвали   хвали-те

Imperfect.

Sg. 1 хваљ-а-х   Pl. хваљ-а-с-мо
   2 хваљ-а-ш-е   хваљ-а-с-те
   3 хваљ-а-ш-е   хваљ-а-х-у

Pres. Part. Act. хваљећи.

Fifth class.

a-Stems.

First group.

чува, *to guard*.

α) inf. stem чува; inf. чува-ти; past part. act.¹ I чува-в, чува-в-ши; II чува-о; past part. passive чува-н.

Aorist.

Sg.	1 чува-х	Pl. чува-с-мо
	2 чува	чува-с-те
	3 чува	чува-ш-е

β) present stem чува-је.

Present.

Sg.	1 чува-м	Pl. чува-мо
	2 чува-ш	чува-те
	3 чува	чува-ју

Imperative.

Sg.	1	Pl. чува-ј-мо
	2 чува-ј	чува-ј-те

Imperfect.

Sg.	1 чува-х	Pl. чува-с-мо
	2 чува-ш-е	чува-с-те
	3 чува-ш-е	чува-х-у

Pres. Part. Act. чува-ј-ући.

Second group.

писа, *to write*.

α) inf. stem писа; inf. писа-ти; past part. act. I писа-в, пуса-в-ши; II писа-о; past part. passive писан.

Aorist.

Sg.	1 писа-х	Pl. писа-с-мо
	2 писа	писа-с-те
	3 писа	писа-ш-е

β) present stem пиш-е.

PRESENT.

Sg. 1 пиш-е-м   Pl. пиш-е-мо
2 пиш-е-ш   пиш-е-те
3 пиш-е   пиш-у

IMPERATIVE.

Sg. 1   Pl. пиш-и-мо
2 пиш-и   пиш-и-те

IMPERFECT.

Sg. 1 писа-х   Pl. писа-с-мо
2 писа-ш-е   писа-с-те
3 писа-ш-е   писа-х-у

PRES. PART. ACT. пиш-ући.

Third group.

бра, *to collect*.

α) inf. stem бра; inf. бра-ти; past part. act. I брав, бравши; II брао; past part. passive бра-н.

AORIST.

Sg. 1 бра-х   Pl. бра-с-мо
2 бра   бра-с-те
3 бра   бра-ш-е

β) present stem бер-е.

PRESENT.

Sg. 1 бер-е-м   Pl. бер-е-мо
2 бер-е-ш   бер-е-те
3 бер-е   бер-у

IMPERATIVE.

Sg. 1   Pl. бер-и-мо
2 бер-и   бер-и-те

CONJUGATION WITH THE PRESENT SUFFIX.

Imperfect.

Sg. 1 бра̂х   Pl. бра-с-мо
     2 бра-ш-е   бра-с-те
     3 бра-ш-е   бра-х-у

Pres. Part. Act. бер-ykи.

Fourth group.

cêja, *to sow*.(¹)

α) inf. stem сија; inf. сија-ти; past part. act. I сија-в, сија-в-ши; II сијао; past part. passive сија-н.

Aorist.

Sg. 1 сија-х   Pl. сија-с-мо
     2 сија   сија-с-те
     3 сија   сија-ш-е

β) present stem си-j-e.

Present.

Sg. 1 си-j-е-м   Pl. си-j-е-мо
     2 си-j-е-ш   си-j-е-те
     3 си-j-е   си-j-у

Imperative.

Sg. 1   Pl. си-j-мо
     2 сиj   си-j-те

Imperfect.

Sg. 1 си-j-a-х   Pl. си-j-a-с-мо
     2 си-j-a-ш-е   си-j-a-с-те
     3 си-j-a-ш-е   си-j-a-х-у

Pres. Part. Act. си-j-ykи.

(¹) The ê correspond to the old Slavonic ѣ.

Sixth class.

ova (ua)-Stems.

a) inf. stem купова; inf. купова-ти; past part. act. I куповав, купова-в-ши; II купова-о; past part. pass. купован.

Aorist.

Sg. 1 купова-х   Pl. купова-с-мо
    2 купова   купова-с-те
    3 купова   купова-ш-е

β) present stem купу-j-е.

Present.

Sg. 1 купу-j-е-м   Pl. купу-j-е-мо
    2 купш-j-е-ш   купу-j-е-те
    3 купу-j-е   купу-j-у

Imperatif.

Sg. 1   Pl. купу-j-мо
    2 купу-j-е   купу-j-те

Imperfect.

Sg. 1 купова-х   Pl. купова-с-мо
    2 купова-ш-е   купова-с-те
    3 купова-ш-е   купова-х-у

Pres. Part. Act. купу-j-ући.

B.—CONJUGATION WITHOUT THE PRESENT SUFFIX.

1. вêд, to know.[1]

Present.

Sg. 1 ви-м   Pl. ви-мо
    2 ви-ш   ви-тс
    3 ви   ви-jу

---

[1] By the addition of these forms the Serbian verb is brought into harmony with the old Slavonic system; ê corresponds to the old Slavonic ѣ. The forms of the root вêд are only found in Serbian with prefixes; e. g. повиj. The infinitive is wanting and is supplied by знати and умјети, but Slovenish helps us to fill of the gap and gives both vediti and vědĕti (Šuman, *Slovenska Slovnica*, p. 161).

CONJUGATION WITHOUT THE PRESENT SUFFIX.

Imperative.

Sg. 1   Pl. вијмо
    2   виј   вијте

2. дад (дати), *to give.*

Present.

Sg. 1   да-м   Pl. да-мо
    2   да-ш   да-те
    3   да   дад-у

Imperative.

Sg. 1   Pl. дaj-мо
    2   дaj   дaj-те

3. jèд (jести), *to eat.*(¹)

Present.

Sg. 1   иje-м   Pl. иje-мо
    2   иje-ш   иje-те
    3   иje   иjy

Imperative.

Sg. 1   Pl. jeди-мо
    2   jeди   jeди-те

4. jec, *to be.*(²)

Present.

Sg. 1   jec-а-м   Pl. jec-мо
    2   je-си   jec-те
    3   jec-т   jec-у

* The present tense is shortened into сам, си, je, смо, сте, су and with the negation нисам, ниси, &c.

(¹) In the Serbian dialect strictly so called the initial и of this tense is omitted.

(²) For practical purposes this tense is given over again on page 51 in the full paradigm of the verb бити, *to be.*

The Serbian verb has the following moods:—Indicative, imperative, conditional and infinitive. It has also the following tenses: the present, the imperfect (not much used in ordinary conversation), the aorist, the perfect, the pluperfect, the past anterior, the simple future, the future anterior.

It will thus be seen that there are many compound tenses, and the mode of forming these will be given, before we proceed to the paradigms of the complete verb.

The auxiliaries are хотјети or хтети, хоћу, *will*, and бити, *to be*.

A.—With the auxiliary хотјети is formed the simp'e future by abridging the present of that verb, and adding it to the infinitive of the verb, the sense of which it is to modify, thus we get ћу, ћеш &c. я ћу чинити, or more frequently in the contracted form чинити ћу. Also би ћеш, *thou wilt be*, for бити ћеш; cf. also хвали ћеш, плеш ћеш which are generally written as one word. The full form is used in interrogative propositions and the corresponding answers, *e. g.* хоћеш ли доћи са мном, *will you come with me*; хоћу, *I will come*.

B.—The use of бити is far more elaborate and the following tenses are formed from it.

1) The perfect, which is formed by the present of the verb бити, and the second past participle active, which is inflected -ао, -ла, -ло for the singular and -ли for plural, as ја сам пао or пао сам, *I have fallen*; Г. Ристић је потпуно успио, *M. Ristich has completely succeeded*.

2) The pluperfect, which is formed by the imperfect of the auxiliary verb and the second past participle; as бијах or бјех чинио, *I had done*.

3) The past anterior, which is formed by the perfect of the auxiliary and the second past participle of the verb, as ja сам био чинио, *I had done.*

4) The future anterior formed by the simple future and the second past participle of the verb, as ja ћу бит учинио, *I shall have done.*

5) The present conditional is formed by adding the aorist бих of the auxiliary to the second past participle, as ja бих чинио, *I should do.* Cf. English 'If I were to do'.

6) The past conditional is formed by adding the past participle of the auxiliary, био, with the aorist бих to the second past participle, as био бих пао, *I should have fallen.*

7) The compound future of the conditional which is formed by the simple future of the auxiliary added to the second past participle of the verb, as ако будем пао, *in case I shall have fallen.* The infinitive may also be equally used, as ако будем пасти.

8) The past infinitive is expressed by the aid of the present infinitive of the auxiliary and the second past participle of the verb;—*e. g.* бити чинио, *to have done.*

9) The third persons singular and plural of the imperative are the same as the third persons singular and plural of the present indicative with the prefix of нека.

The full conjugation of the verb бити, *to be,* is here given on account of its importance as an auxiliary.

(¹) Its formation by the help of the infinitive seems to be more in use among the Croats than the Serbs.

Present Tense.

Singular.	Plural.
јесам or сам, *I am*	јесмо or смо, *we are*
јеси or си, *thou art*	јесте or сте, *you are*
јест or је, *he is*	јесу or су, *they are*

Imperfect.

Singular.	Plural.
бијах (or бјех), *I was*, or бих	бијасмо, бјесмо, *we were*, or бисмо
бијаше, бјеше, *thou wast*, or би	бијасте, бјесте, *you were*, or бисте
бијаше, бјеше, *he was*, or би	бијаху, бјеху, *they were*, or бише

Aorist.

Singular.	Plural.
бих	бисмо
би	бисте
би	бише

Perfect.

Singular.

ја сам, *I have*
ти си, *thou hast* } био, била, било, *been*
он, она, оно је, *he has*

Plural.

ми смо, *we have*
ви сте, *you have* } били, -е, -а, *been*
они, оне, она су, *they have*

Future.

Singular.	Plural.
будем, *I shalt be*	будемо, *we shall be*
будеш, *thou shall be*	будете, *you shall be*
буде, *he shall be*	буду, *they shall be*

THE VERB.

Imperative.

Singular.
буди, *be thou*
нека буде, *let him be*

Plural.
будимо, *let us be*
будите, *be ye*
нека буду, *let them be*

INFINITIVE: бити, *to be.*
PARTICIPLES: бивши, *having been.*
PAST: био, ла, ло, *been.*
FUTURE: будући, *being.*

The past participle is used in composition to express a condition, cf. our were I that, I should go, &c.

NOTE.—The prefix не which is often joined to Serbian verbs and gives a negative sense, becomes ни in the present tense of the verb бити, as ни-јесам, *contracted*, нисам, &c.

Besides the forms already given in the fully conjugated verb, some grammarians have assigne a supine to the Serbian verb; this however is declared by MIKLOSICH (Vergl. Gramm. III, 225) to have been long out of use.

The present tense of the verb хотјети is here added as it is used as an auxiliary to express the future.

Singular.
1. хоћу or ћу
2. хоћеш or ћеш
3. хоће or ће

Plural.
хоћемо or ћемо
хоћете or ћете
хоће or ће

Negative Form.

Singular.
нећу
нећеш
неће

Plural.
нећемо
нећете
неће

PARADIGM OF A COMPLETE VERB.(¹)

A.—ACTIVE VOICE.

Present.

Singular.	Plural.
хвалим, *I praise*	хвалимо, *we praise*
хвалиш, *thou praisest*	хвалите, *you praise*
хвали, *he praises*	хвале, *they praise*

Imperfect.

Singular.	Plural.
ваљах, *I was praising*	хваљасмо, *we were praising*
хваљаше, *thou wast praising*	хваљасте, *you were praising*
хваљаше, *he was praising*	хваљаху, *they were praising*

Aorist.

Singular.	Plural.
хвалих, *I praised*	хвалисмо, *we praised*
хвали, *thou didst praise*	хвалисте, *ye praised*
хвали, *he praised*	хвалише, *they praised*

Perfect.

Singular.
јесам, сам хвалио, *I have praised*
јеси, си хвалио, *thou hast praised*
јест, је хвалио, *he has praised*

Plural.
јесмо, смо хвалили, *we have praised*
јесте, сте хвалили, *ye have praised*
јесу, су хвалили, *they have praised*

(¹) As the verbal suffixes have already been marked they are not specified on this occasion.

THE VERB.

Pluperfect.

Singular.

бијах (бјех) хвалио, *I had praised*
бијаше (бјеше) хвалио, *thou hadst praised*
бијаше (бјеше) хвалио, *he had praised*

Plural.

бијасмо (бјесмо) хвалили, *we had praised*
бијасте (бјесте) хвалили, *you had praised*
бијаху (бјеху) хвалили, *they had praised*

Past Anterior.

Singular.

био сам хвалио, *I had praised*
био си хвалио, *thou hadst praised*
био је хвалио, *he had praised*

Plural.

били смо хвалили, *we had praised*
били сте хвалили, *ye had praised*
били су хвалили, *they had praised*[1]

Future Simple.

Singular.

хвалит ћу, *I shall praise*
хвалит ћеш, *thou shalt praise*
хвалит ће, *he shall praise*

Plural.

хвалит ћемо, *we shall praise*
хвалит ћете, *ye shall praise*
хвалит ће, *they shall praise*

---

[1] The arrangement is altered, if the personal pronoun is introduced:—thus the order would be ja сам био хвалио, &c. So also in the future simple it would be ja ћу хвалити, &c., and the present conditional without the personal pronouns would be хвалио бих.

Future anterior.

Singular.

бит ћу хвалио, *I shall have praised*
бит ћеш хвалио, *thou shalt have praised*
бит ће хвалио, *he shall have praised*

Plural.

бит ћемо хвалили, *we shall have praised*
бит ћете хвалили, *ye shall have praised*
бит ће хвалили, *they shall have praised*

Conditional-Mood.

Present.

Singular.

ја бих хвалио, *I should praise*(¹)
ти би хвалио, *thou shouldst praise*
он би хвалио, *he should praise*

Plural.

ми бисмо хвалили, *we should praise*
ви бисте хвалили, *you should praise*
они би хвалили, *they should praise*

Past.

Singular.

био бих хвално, *I should have praised*
био би хвалио, *thou shouldst have praised*
био би хвалио, *he should have praised*

Plural.

били бисмо хвалили, *we should have praised*
били бисте хвалили, *you should have praised*
били би хвалили, *they should have praised*

(¹) The personal pronouns are sometimes omitted in the case of verbs, when they are not wanted for clearness or emphasis. They have, therefore, not been given with all the tenses.

Future simple.
Singular.
уз-хвалим, *if I shall praise*
уз-хвалиш, *if thou shalt praise*
уз-хвали, *if he shall praise*

Plural.
уз-хвалимо, *if we shall praise*
уз-хвалите, *if ye shall praise*
уз-хвале, *if they shall praise*

The prefix here gives a future meaning to an imperfect verb and the practice of the Slavonic languages of introducing compound forms into simple verbs, where some tenses in simple verbs are deficient has been previously explained on page 34. By this prefix an imperfective verb is made perfective. The prefix, the use of which MIKLOSICH compares with the Greek ἀνά is employed to make an imperfective verb perfective. It is only employed in dependent sentences and only with this tense. Thus cf. Matthew 5, 11. Благо вама ако вас узасрамоте и успрогоне и реку на вас свакојаке ръаве ријечи, *blessed are ye when men shall revile you and persecute you and shall say all manner of evil against you.*

This tense is always used with a conjunction, as да, ако, кад, нека

Compound future.
Singular.
будем хвалио, (*if*) *I shall have praised*
будеш хвалио, (*if*) *thou shalt have praised*
буде хвалио, (*if*) *he shall have praised*

Plural.
будемо хвалили, (*if*) *we shall have praised*
будете хвалили, (*if*) *you shall have praised*
буду хвалили, (*if*) *they shall have praised*

Imperative.

Singular.	Plural.
	хвалимо, *let us praise*
хвали, *praise thou*	хвалите, *praise ye*
нека хвали, *let him praise*	нека хвале, *let them praise*

Inf. Pres.: хвалити, *to praise.*
Inf. Past: бити хвалио, *to have praised.*
Part. Pres.: хвалећи, -a, -e, *praising.*
I. Part. Past: хваливши, -a, -e, *having praised.*
II. Part. Past: хвалио, -ла, -ло, *praised.*
Pass. Part. Past: хваљен, -a, -o, *praised.* (¹)
Gerund Pres.: хвалећ(и), *praising.*
Gerund Past: хвалив(ши), *having praised.*

Each verb has its verbal noun, as чување, *the act of watching*; пјевање, *the singing.*

B.—THE PASSIVE VOICE.

This may be expressed by the past participle passive of the verb with the auxiliary бити, but this form is very rarely used by the Serbs. It is generally expressed by the active with the relative се, as не судите да вам се не суди, *judge not that ye be not judged.*

It may be said of the Slavonic languages generally that they abhor passive forms.

Impersonal Verbs.

Such are
дажди, *it rains,*
грми, *it thunders,*
снежи, *it snows.*

(¹) Serbian, like Malo-Russian and Polish has no present participle passive.

Some are reflexive, as

дани се, *it begins to dawn*,
смркава се, *it grows dark*.

Sometimes personal verbs are used impersonally by an idiom in which all the Slavonic languages share, as

спи ми се, *I sleep*,
треба ми се, *I have need*,
хоће, неће ми се, *I wish, I do not wish*.

There are certain other idiomatic uses of impersonal verbs, the knowledge of which must be acquired by practice;—*e. g.* срди ме, *it makes me feel angry*; жао ми је, *I am sorry*; може, as може се добити у књижари, *it may be procured from the booksellers.* Very frequent is the impersonal use of нема or није, as in other Slavonic languages, as нема среће код куће, *there is no prosperity at home.*

IRREGULAR VERBS.

A few remarks on some irregular verbs in constant use are here added for the benefit of the student.

Ткати, *to weave*, makes in the present tense ткам, ткем and чем.

Спати, *to sleep*, makes in the present спим.

To the second class of stems without suffixes belongs the irregular verb нести, for the aorist the forms несох, нијех occur. The past participle active II is нио, њела, but sometimes несао, несла, ло; ити (ићи), *to go*, has the following forms:

Present.

идем or идеш &c. (ићем, еш &c.).

Imperfect.

идах or идијах,
идаше or идијаше (ићах, ићаше).

Aorist.

идох or иде (ићох or иће).

Imperative.

иди, идите (ићи, ићите).
Pres. Participle: идући.
Past Part. Active I: ишавши (идавши).
Past Part. Active II: ишао, ишла, ишло. (¹)
Passive Participle: ићен, а, о (ишаст, а, о).

Гнати, *to hunt*, *a*-stems, No. 3, makes in present женем, also пенем and sometimes гнам.

ADVERBS.

The Serbian language in this respect does not exhibit any peculiarities. The ordinary termination of the adverb when derived from the adjective is -o, as добро, *well*. A few specimens of each kind of adverb are given here, but the learner will easily get them from the dictionary.

Those adverbs which are derived from adjectives have a comparative and superlative;—the comparative ending in -ије and the superlative being formed by the addition of нај or пре, as весело, *merrily*, веселије, *more merrily*, највеселије or превесело, *most merrily*.

(¹) Russian шёлъ, шла, шло, the initial vowel being lost.

ADVERBS.

Adverbs of Manner.

како, *as*, тако, *so*,
пјешке, *on foot*, врло, *very*.

Among these adverbs besides those formed from adjectives, certain adverbial expressions formed by a preposition and a noun must be included, as из ненада, *unexpectedly*; из тиха, *slowly*; с мјеста, *straight away* and others. Many end in -ски derived from adjectives, as француски, *in the French way*; господски, *as a master*.

Adverbs of Quantity.

довољно, *enough*, обилно, *abundantly*,
мало, *a little*, ништа, *nothing*,
више, *more*, тек, *a little*.

Adverbs of Place.

близу, *near*, около, *around*,
доли, *below*, скроз, *through*,
тамо амо, *here and there*,
преко, *across*.

Adverbs of Time.

брзо, *quickly*, давно, *long ago*,
рано, *early*, већ, *already*,
скоро, *quickly*, сада, *now*,
кашто, *sometimes*, ноћу, *during the night*.

Interrogative Adverbs.

где, *where*; јер, зашто, *why*.

Affirmative.

да, *yes*; заиста, *surely*.

Negation.

не, *not*; никако, *in no way*.

Doubt.

ако, да, *if*; једа, *perhaps*; једва, *hardly*.

PREPOSITIONS.

A few of the leading prepositions will be given here with the cases which they govern.

The following take the genitive:
без, *without*,
пут, *towards*,
ради, *for the sake of*,
до, *up to*,
мјесто, *in place of*,
усред, *in the midst*.

The following take the dative:
к, то, проти, *against*.

The following take the accusative:
кроз, *through*; уз, *up*.

The following takes the locative alone:
при, *by the side of*.

The following take the genitive and instrumental:
с, са, су, *with*.

The following take the genitive and dative:
против, супрот, *against*.

The following take the accusative and instrumental in so far as they indicate movement or repose:
мед, међу, *among*; над, *on*; под, *under*; пред, *before*.

The following take the accusative and locative:
на, *on*; о, *concerning*; по, *after*.

The following takes the genitive, accusative and locative:
у, *in* or *at*.

The following takes the genitive, accusative and instrumental:
за, *behind* or *for*, ая служи за предбројбу, *it is as good as a subscription*.

CONJUNCTIONS.

Copulative:

и, *and*; такођер, *in the same manner*; не само — него и, *not only — but.*

Disjunctive:

а.ш, и.ш or буд — буд, *whether — or.*

Adversative:

а.ш, но, *but*; са свим тим, *for all that*; него, *than*, as боље је знати, него имати, *it is better to know than to possess.*

Causative:

јер, јеро, *because that*; да, *in order that*; па, *and then*, as вукодлак, човјек, кој послије смрти устане и хода у сподоби вука па сиса људем крв, *vampire, a man who rises after death and goes in the likeness of a wolf and then sucks men's blood.*

Interrogative:

.ш, да.ш, ја.ш, *or is it?*

INTERJECTIONS.

It will suffice here to give a few which are especially note-worthy, such as јаох, *alas*; хопа цупа, used to mark the step in the коло or national dance of Serbia, рутине и путине, *nonsense*; с пута, *get out of the way.* The Serbian language is very rich in onomatopœia, and has a series of verbs formed from interjections, and natural cries, as in English, many of which are very expressive, thus цвркутати, *to warble* (as birds), хржити, *to neigh*, &c.

Part III:—SYNTAX.

The Noun.

The genitive case is used after:

a) the verb when it has a partitive sense, as дајте ми круха, *give me some bread.*

b) the verb when there is a negative in the sentence, as сребра и злата нема у мепе (Acts III, 6), *silver and gold I have none.*

c) to express point of time, but the instrumental is more often used; thus у Оксфорду десетога студна тисућу осам сто осамдесет и пет, *Oxford the tenth of November* (lit. cold month) 1885.

d) when the numerals два, три, четири and оба are undeclined, the noun after them is put in the genitive singular(¹), but from пет onwards it is in the genitive plural.

e) after some adjectives, especially denoting immunity from, the preposition од being also employed, as чист од љаге, *exempt from fault*; прост гриеха and од гриеха, *exempt from sin.*

f) with од the genitive is used after the comparative and superlative of adjectives, as је ли што шире од мора, је ли што слађе од меда, *is there any thing broader*

(¹) The rule is the same in Russian. Miklosich thinks that it is the remains of an old dual form, and a genitive singular only in appearance. This seems to be proved by the fact that if an adjective accompanies the noun it is put in what has been called the neuter plural, but in reality is a dual два велика храста, *two great oaks.*

than the sea, is there any thing sweeter than honey.— Superlative: најсилнији од свих владара, *the most powerful of all monarchs,* sometimes него is used, as моја је башта лепша(¹) него твоја, *my garden is prettier than thine.*

g) verbs implying to deliver, or separate from, frequently with the preposition од, as чувати кога чеса or од чеса, *to guard any one from anything*; ослободити кога чеса, *to deliver,* &c.

h) implying memory, as споменути кога чеса, *to remind any one of a thing.*

i) implying request or acquirement which take the genitive with у, as питати што у кога, *to ask anything of a person*; добити што у кога, *to gain anything,* &c.

The Dative case is used after:

a) adjectives implying advantage, or experience and the contrary, as благ кому, *agreeable to any one*; неук чему, *ignorant of anything*; злочест кому, *mischievous to any one.*

b) after verbs implying to give or to do anything profitable to a person, as дати кому што, *to give anything to a person*; бранити кому што, *to defend a person against anything*; учити кога чему, *to teach a person anything.* As in Latin we get даровати кога чим and кому што.

c) to tell to any one, to rule, to threaten, to thank &c., as казати кому, *to narrate to any one*; господовати кому, *to rule any one*; пристити кому, *to threaten* &c.; захва-

---

(¹) Irregular comparative of лјеп or леп, *beautiful.*

E

лити кому, *to thank*; обикнути чему, *to accustom oneself to anything.*

d) many impersonals and reflexives;—*e. g.* молити се. кому, *to pray to any one.* (¹)

The accusative is used after:

a) verbs, as the common case of expressing the object.

b) The accusative is used to mark extent or dimension, both of time and place and is sometimes used for point of time with the preposition у, as у петак, *on Friday.*

The instrumental case is used:

a) as the regular case to express the agent or instrument, as

   Они ће ми одмаздити
   Мојом главом влашке главе
*They will make me atone
By means of my head for the heads of the Wallachs.*
       Ivan Mažuranić.
    Smrt Čengić-age, line 12.

b) it is used after certain adjectives implying riches, content &c.;—*e. g.* богат чим, *rich in something*; довољан чим, *content with something.* So also плодан, *fertile*; славан, *celebrated*; велик, *great*, &c.

(¹) For many other peculiar constructions of the verbs the reader must be recommended to use a good dictionary: the knowledge of them can only be acquired by practice. Unfortunately a Serbo-English dictionary is still a *desideratum*, and the student must betake himself to German aids.

c) There is also what has been appropriately called the *predicative* use of this case when it is employed after verbs of appointing, nominating &c., as Стефан постане зетом султана, *Stephen becomes the sultan's son-in-law*; изабрати кога краљем, *to elect any one king*; именовати тајником, *to name any one private secretary*.

d) It is also sometimes used to express point of time, as Сријед̣ом и Суботом долази пошта, *the Post arrives Wednesday and Saturday*.

THE VERB.

The syntax of the verb has already been partly explained. It only remains to add a few peculiarities.

In the imperative instead of the third person singular, the second is often used, as недај Бог, *may God forbid*.

Instead of the infinitive after a verb we frequently find the indicative used with the conjunction да;—*e. g.* ко има уши да чује, нека чује, *he who has ears to hear let him hear*. So also Acts I, 25 из кога испаде Јуда да иде на мјесто своје, *from which Judas fell that he might go into his own place*. We may compare with this tendency the condition of the Bulgarian and Modern Greek languages in which the infinitive has entirely disappeared.

As in other Slavonic languages, we have the neuter past participle passive used with a case, the accusative of the object, with which MIKLOSICH (IV, 365) very rightly compares such expressions as the Greek ἀσκητέον ἐστὶ τὴν ἀρετήν.

According to PARČIĆ and other writers of Serbian Grammar there is a supine in Serbian: this however is

E*

denied by MIKLOSICH (see Vol. III, p. 225) who appears to regard it as identical with the infinitive.(¹)

The difference between the gerunds and the participles, is that the former are indeclinable, but the latter are declined throughout like adjectives.

SERBIAN READING LESSON.

An extract is here given from the writings of J. SUBBOTIĆ(²), with an interlinear translation which it is hoped may convey to the reader some idea of the Serb syntax.

 Србске народне пјесме и њихов уплив у књижевни
 The Serbian national songs and their influence on written
језик србаљах.
language of the Serbians.

 Издавна јошт живила су јуначка дјела отацах
 For a long time still have lived the heroic deeds of (their) fathers
и праотацах у пјесмама, које у свом роду пара себи
and grandfathers in songs which in their kind an equal to themselve
 траже. Јунаци косовске битке живили
demand (in vain). The heroes of the Kosovo battle have lived
су кроз те пјесме у спомену народа тако
through these songs in (the) memory of the people as

(¹) BERLIĆ says that in Serbian it is constantly confused with the infinitive, and is practically unrecognised (*Grammatik der illirischen Sprache* p. 179).

(²) I have thought it better to let this extract remain with its various dialectical peculiarities both in orthography and grammar. The student must be familiarised with all forms of the Serbo-Croatian language. The addition of -х to the genitive plural must be noticed, as Србаљах, отацах. It is now generally rejected and has therefore not been inserted among the forms of the substantives.

живахно, као да су свима лично познати и да су прије
freshly as if, they were to all personally known and before
неколико годинах поумирали.
some years (they) had died.

Па онај исти кој је пјесме о старима
For this very (reason) he who (the) songs concerning the old ones
најбоље пјевао, опјевао је и јуначка дјела суврјеменаках
best sang, sang also the heroic deeds of contemporaries
својих, који су за крст частни и за домовину крв
his, who for the cross noble and for (their) country blood
проливали, живот изгубили. Ове пјесме прелазиле су од отацах на
shed life lost. These songs came from fathers to
синове и примале су свагда онај образ језика, кој је код
sons and took always that form of language, which among
живећег рода у обичају био; и тако су оне пјесме, које
living people in custom was; and so are those songs which
о најудаљенијем врјемену гласе, по језику сасвим
concerning most remote time speak in language altogether
равне са онима, које догађај нашег времена опјевају.
resembling those which an occurrence of our time sing.

Но значају србског народа сигурно се
Concerning the nature of the Serbian people clearly itself to
узети даје и по свједочбама грчких
apprehend (it) gives and according to the testimonies of the Greek
историках знамо, да је у врјеме краљевах и Царевах
historians we know, that in the time of the Kings and Emperors
србских доста пјесамах било, у којима је народ своје јунаке
Serb many of songs there was, in which the people its heroes
опјевао. Од оних је пјесамах изузимајући Лазарев круг, мало-
sang. From these songs, excepting the Lazarus-cycle, little
њих до нас одржано. Види се, да је катастрофа косово
of them to us is preserved. It is clear that the catastrophe of the
пољска на народ србски страшно утицање имала. Чини
field of Kosovo on the people Serb terrible influence had. It
се, као ди су старци и старе баке овим ударом потре-
seems that the old men and old women by that blow fright-
шени на све друго заборавили, и дјеци и унуцима
ened everything else forgot and to children and grandchildren
својима само о косовом пољу те о косовом пољу и његовим
their only of Kosovo field and of Kosovo field and its
јунацима говорили, и час бољу и несрјећу, час
heroes . spoke and at times the hurt and misfortune, at times

славу	и	величину	тога дана казивали. Силом, великолепосћу,
the glory and grandeur of that day told. By force, grandeur,

важносћу	несрјећом	и	посљедицом	превазилази косовска
importance unhappiness and its consequences exceeds the Kosovo

битка све догађаје, који су прије ње на народ дјеловали.
battle all events, which before this on the people had acted.

Послје	ужасне смрти најмилостивијег од свиух Србских владатељах
After (the) terrible death of the dearest of all Serbian rulers

наиђе на	србски	народ грозна бједа	и невоља,	плод
came on (the) Serbian people horrible poverty and slavery the fruit

унутрашњег раздора	и турског господства.	Бјесни освојн-
of interior disturbance and Turkish rule. The devilish con-

тељи	разтјерају прије свега властелство, или га сваког права
querors destroyed before all the nobility, or their every right

лише,	да тако кости из тјела	народа	извуку,
took away, just as if bones from the body of (the) people they took,

да се на њима	држати	неможе:	бездушним глобљењем
so that on them support itself it could not. By heartless plundering

лише	народ	имања,	да га	тим
it deprives *the people of (their) property, so that them thereby

мирнијим и подашијим	учише;	заузму	му
humble and subject it should make; they took away from them

градове и већа мјеста, да га	боље	под
(their) towns and greater cities, so that them (the people) better under

уздом држати	могу, и њега одтјерају у	горе	и долине.
the bridle keep they might and them drove to the mountain and valley.

Но тим му учине	оно, што су најмање	хтјели,
But by this to them they did that, which least of all they wished,

и што му се само најбоље учинити могло; тим су га
and which to them only best to do was possible, by this them

натјерали,	да несмјешан остане. да се	њима напроти
they compelled unmixed to remain, to make them against (them)

стави и да собствено тјело чини,	пак да се позна са
stand and a peculiar body to form, so that they made them

	гором	и грмом, који ће	му
acquainted with the mountain and the oak which could to them

после	непредобитни бедеми бити.
afterwards insuperable barriers be.

From this extract a fair idea may be formed of the construction of a sentence in the Serbian language. As it is in a highly synthetic state great variety is allowed; the order on the whole is the natural one, and the Slavonic languages are free from the cumbrous and pedantic sentences of the German and other tongues. The verb is frequently, but not necessarily, put at the end of a period. The adjective and participle can be separated by many words from the substantives with which they agree, as may be seen in the passages taken from SUBBOTIĆ.

A CATALOGUE

OF

EDUCATIONAL WORKS

PUBLISHED BY

KEGAN PAUL, TRENCH, TRÜBNER, & CO. L^TD

PATERNOSTER HOUSE, CHARING CROSS ROAD.

CONTENTS.

	PAGE		PAGE		PAGE
ALBANIAN	1	GREEK	13	PORTUGUESE	20
ANGLO-SAXON	1	HUNGARIAN	14	ROUMANIAN	21
BASQUE	2	INTERNATIONAL LAN-		RUSSIAN	21
DANO-NORWEGIAN	2	GUAGES	14	SERBIAN	22
DUTCH	3	ITALIAN	14	SPANISH	22
ENGLISH AND		LATIN	15	SWEDISH	23
GENERAL	3	NORWEGIAN—see		TECHNOLOGICAL DIC-	
FRENCH	8	DANO-NORWEGIAN.		TIONARIES	23
FRISIAN	11	ORIENTAL	15	TURKISH	24
GERMAN	11	POLISH	19		

ALBANIAN.

GRAMMAIRE ALBANAISE à l'Usage de ceux qui désirent apprendre cette Langue sans l'Aide d'un Maître Par P. W. Crown 8vo. 7s. 6d.

ANGLO-SAXON.

HARRISON and BASKERVILL. HANDY DICTIONARY OF ANGLO-SAXON POETRY. Based on Groschopp's Grein. Edited, Revised, and Corrected, with Grammatical Appendix, List of Irregular Verbs, and Brief Etymological Features. By JAMES A. HARRISON, Professor of English and Modern Languages in Washington and Lee University, Virginia; and W. M. BASKERVILL, Ph.D. Lips., Professor of English Language and Literature in Vanderbilt University, Nashville, Ten. Square 8vo. 12s.

MARCH. COMPARATIVE GRAMMAR OF THE ANGLO-SAXON LANGUAGE; in which its forms are illustrated by those of the Sanskrit, Greek, Latin, Gothic, Old Saxon, Old Friesic, Old Norse, and Old High German. By FRANCIS A. MARCH, LL.D. 8vo. 10s.

A

MARCH. INTRODUCTION TO ANGLO-SAXON. An Anglo-Saxon Reader. With Philological Notes, a Brief Grammar, and a Vocabulary. By FRANCIS A. MARCH, LL.D. 8vo. 7s. 6d.

RASK. GRAMMAR OF THE ANGLO-SAXON TONGUE, from the Danish of Erasmus Rask. By BENJAMIN THORPE. Third Edition, Corrected and Improved, with Plate. Post 8vo. 5s. 6d.

WRIGHT. ANGLO-SAXON AND OLD ENGLISH VOCABULARIES. By THOMAS WRIGHT, M.A., F.S.A., Hon. M.R.S.L. Illustrating the Condition and Manners of our Forefathers, as well as the History of the Forms of Elementary Education, and of the Languages Spoken in this Island from the Tenth Century to the Fifteenth. Second Edition, Edited and Collated by RICHARD PAUL WULCKER. 2 vols. 8vo. 28s.

BASQUE.

VAN EYS. OUTLINES OF BASQUE GRAMMAR. By W. J VAN EYS. Crown 8vo. 3s. 6d.]

DANO-NORWEGIAN.

BOJESEN. GUIDE TO THE DANISH LANGUAGE. Designed for English Students. By Mrs. MARIA BOJESEN. 12mo 5s.

LARSEN. DANISH-ENGLISH DICTIONARY. By L. LARSEN. Crown 8vo. 10s. 6d.

OTTÉ. DANO-NORWEGIAN GRAMMAR: A Manual for Students of Danish, based on the Ollendorffian System of Teaching Languages, and adapted for Self-Instruction. By E. C. OTTÉ. Second Edition. Crown 8vo. 7s. 6d. Key, 3s.

OTTÉ. SIMPLIFIED GRAMMAR OF THE DANISH LANGUAGE. By E. C. OTTÉ. Crown 8vo. 2s. 6d.

POCKET DICTIONARY OF THE ENGLISH AND DANO-NORWEGIAN-LANGUAGES. 2 parts, bound in 1 vol. [18mo. 5s. 6d.

ROSING. ENGLISH-DANISH DICTIONARY. By S. ROSING. Crown 8vo. 8s. 6d.

SMITH and HORNEMAN. NORWEGIAN GRAMMAR; with a Glossary for Tourists. By M. SMITH and H. HORNEMAN. Post 8vo. 2s.

DUTCH.

AHN. CONCISE GRAMMAR OF THE DUTCH LANGUAGE, with Selections from the Best Authors in Prose and Poetry. After Dr. F. AHN'S Method. Fourth Edition, thoroughly Revised and Enlarged by Dr. J. M. HOOGVLIET and Dr. KERN (of Leiden). 12mo. 3s. 6d.

KRAMERS. NEW POCKET-DICTIONARY OF THE ENGLISH-DUTCH AND DUTCH-ENGLISH LANGUAGES. Containing also in the First Part Pronunciation, and a Vocabulary of Proper Names, Geographical and Historical. By J. KRAMERS. 16mo. 4s.

PICARD. NEW POCKET-DICTIONARY OF THE ENGLISH-DUTCH AND DUTCH-ENGLISH LANGUAGES. Remodelled and Corrected from the best Authorities. By A. PICARD. Fifth Edition. 16mo. 10s.

ENGLISH AND GENERAL.

ABEL. LINGUISTIC ESSAYS. By CARL ABEL. Post 8vo. 9s.

ABEL. SLAVIC AND LATIN: Lectures on Comparative Lexicography. By CARL ABEL. Post 8vo. 5s.

ABRAHAMS. MANUAL OF SCRIPTURE HISTORY FOR JEWISH SCHOOLS AND FAMILIES. By L. B. ABRAHAMS. With Map. Crown 8vo. 1s. 6d.

ALLIBONE. DICTIONARY OF ENGLISH LITERATURE AND BRITISH AND AMERICAN AUTHORS, from the Earliest Account to the Latter Half of the 19th Century. By S. A. ALLIBONE. 3 vols. Royal 8vo. £5, 8s.

ANDERSON. PRACTICAL MERCANTILE CORRESPONDENCE. A Collection of Modern Letters of Business, with Notes, Critical and Explanatory, and an Appendix, containing a Dictionary of Commercial Technicalities, pro forma Invoices, Account Sales, Bills of Lading, and Bills of Exchange; also an Explanation of the German Chain Rule. Thirtieth Edition, Revised and Enlarged. By WILLIAM ANDERSON. Crown 8vo. 3s. 6d.

ARMITAGE. LECTURES ON PAINTING, Delivered to the Students of the Royal Academy. By EDWARD ARMITAGE. Crown 8vo. 7s. 6d.

BAIN. EDUCATION AS A SCIENCE. By ALEX. BAIN. Seventh Edition. Crown 8vo. 5s. (International Scientific Series.)

BARNES. GLOSSARY OF THE DORSET DIALECT, with a Grammar of its Word-Shapening and Wording. By WILLIAM BARNES. 8vo. Sewed. 6s.

BARTLETT. DICTIONARY OF AMERICANISMS : A Glossary of Words and Phrases Colloquially Used in the United States. By J. R. BARTLETT. Fourth Edition. 8vo. 21s.

BELL. SOUNDS AND THEIR RELATIONS. A Complete Manual of Universal Alphabets, Illustrated by Means of Visible Speech; and Exhibiting the Pronunciation of English, in Various Styles, and of other Languages and Dialects. By A. MELVILLE BELL, F.E.I.S., &c. 4to. 7s. 6d.

BELL. THE FAULTS OF SPEECH; a Self-Corrector and Teachers' Manual. By A. MELVILLE BELL, F.E.I.S. 18mo. 2s. 6d.

BELL. THE PRINCIPLES OF ELOCUTION, with Exercises and Notations for Pronunciation, Intonation, Emphasis, Gesture, and Emotional Expression. By A. MELVILLE BELL, F.E.I.S., &c. Fourth Revised and Enlarged Edition. 12mo. 7s. 6d.

BELL. VISIBLE SPEECH. The Science of Universal Alphabetics; or, Self-Interpreting Physiological Letters for the Writing of all Languages in One Alphabet. Illustrated by Tables, Diagrams, and Examples. By A. MELVILLE BELL, F.E.I.S., &c. 4to. £1, 5s.

BELL. ENGLISH VISIBLE SPEECH FOR THE MILLION, for Communicating the Exact Pronunciation of the Language to Native and Foreign Learners, and for Teaching Children and Illiterate Adults to Read in a few Days. By A. MELVILLE BELL, F.E.I.S., &c. 4to. Paper, 2s.

BLATER. TABLE OF NAPIER, GIVING THE NINE MULTIPLES OF ALL NUMBERS. By JOSEPH BLATER. Cloth case. 1s. 3d.

BOWEN. STUDIES IN ENGLISH FOR THE USE OF MODERN SCHOOLS. By H. C. BOWEN. Tenth Thousand. Small crown 8vo. 1s. 6d.

BOWEN. ENGLISH GRAMMAR FOR BEGINNERS. By H. C. BOWEN. Fcap. 8vo. 1s.

BOWEN. SIMPLE ENGLISH POEMS. English Literature for Junior Classes. By H. C. BOWEN. 3s. Parts I., II., and III., 6d. each. Part IV., 1s.

BROWNING. INTRODUCTION TO THE HISTORY OF EDUCATIONAL THEORIES. By OSCAR BROWNING. Second Edition. 3s. 6d.

BRUGMANN. COMPARATIVE GRAMMAR OF THE INDO-GERMANIC LANGUAGES. By CARL BRUGMANN. 2 vols. 8vo. 18s. each.

BYRNE. GENERAL PRINCIPLES OF THE STRUCTURE OF LANGUAGE. By JAMES BYRNE. 2 vols. 8vo. 36s.

BYRNE. ORIGIN OF GREEK, LATIN, AND GOTHIC ROOTS. By JAMES BYRNE. 8vo. 18s.

CARREÑO. METODO PARA APRENDER A LEER, Escribir y hablar el Inglés segun el sistema de Ollendorff, con un tratado de pronunciacion al principio y un Apendice importante al fin, que sirve de complemento a la obra. Por RAMON PALENZUELA Y JUAN DE LA CARREÑO. Nueva Edicion, con una Pronunciacion Figurada segun un Sistema Fonografico, por ROBERT GOODACRE. Crown 8vo. 4s. 6d. Key, 3s.

CHARNOCK. NUCES ETYMOLOGICÆ. By R. S. CHARNOCK. Crown 8vo. 10s.

CLODD. CHILDHOOD OF RELIGIONS, including a Simple Account of the Birth and Growth of Myths and Legends. By EDWARD CLODD. New and Revised Edition. Crown 8vo. 5s. Special Edition for Schools, 1s. 6d.

CLODD. CHILDHOOD OF THE WORLD: a Simple Account of Man in Early Times. By EDWARD CLODD. Eighth Edition. Crown 8vo. 3s. Special Edition for Schools, 1s.

CLODD. JESUS OF NAZARETH, with a Brief Sketch of Jewish History to the Time of His Birth. By EDWARD CLODD. Second Edition. Small crown 8vo. 6s. Special Edition for Schools in 2 parts, each 1s. 6d.

COX. TALES OF ANCIENT GREECE. By Sir G. W. COX. New Edition. Small crown 8vo. 6s.

COX. MANUAL OF MYTHOLOGY IN THE FORM OF QUESTION AND ANSWER. By Sir G. W. Cox. New Edition. Fcap. 8vo. 3s.

DANA. TEXT-BOOK OF GEOLOGY, for Schools. By JAMES D. DANA. Illustrated. Crown 8vo. 10s.

DANA. TEXT-BOOK OF MINERALOGY, with Treatise on Crystallography and Physical Mineralogy. By E. S. DANA. Third Edition, with 800 Woodcuts and Plates. 8vo. 15s.

DAWSON. GEOLOGICAL HISTORY OF PLANTS. By Sir J. W. DAWSON. With 80 Figures. Crown 8vo. 5s.

DELBRUCK. INTRODUCTION TO THE STUDY OF LANGUAGE: the History and Methods of Comparative Philology of the Indo-European Languages. By B. DELBRUCK. 8vo. 5s.

GALLOWAY. EDUCATION: SCIENTIFIC AND TECHNICAL; or, How the Inductive Sciences are Taught, and How they Ought to be Taught. By R. GALLOWAY, F.C.S. 8vo. 10s. 6d.

GARLANDA. THE PHILOSOPHY OF WORDS: A Popular Introduction to the Science of Language. By FEDERICO GARLANDA. Crown 8vo. 5s.

GASTER. GREEKO-SLAVONIC LITERATURE AND ITS RELATION TO THE FOLK-LORE OF EUROPE DURING THE MIDDLE AGES. By M. GASTER. Large post 8vo. 7s. 6d.

GOULD. GOOD ENGLISH; or, Popular Errors in Language. By EDWARD S. GOULD. New Edition. Crown 8vo. 6s.

HALDEMAN. PENNSYLVANIA DUTCH : a Dialect of South Germany with an Infusion of English. By S. S. HALDEMAN. 8vo. 3s. 6d.

HODGSON. ACADEMY LECTURES. By J. E. HODGSON. Crown 8vo. 7s. 6d.

HODGSON. THE EDUCATION OF GIRLS ; and the Employment of Women of the Upper Classes Educationally Considered. By W. B. HODGSON. Second Edition. Crown 8vo. 3s. 6d.

HULME. MATHEMATICAL DRAWING INSTRUMENTS, AND HOW TO USE THEM. By F. EDWARD HULME. With Illustrations. Third Edition. Imperial 16mo. 3s. 6d.

JENKINS. VEST-POCKET LEXICON. An English Dictionary of all except Familiar Words, including the Principal Scientific and Technical Terms, and Foreign Moneys, Weights and Measures ; omitting what everybody knows, and containing what everybody wants to know and cannot readily find. By JABEZ JENKINS. 64mo. Roan. 1s. 6d.

LAGRANGE. PHYSIOLOGY OF BODILY EXERCISE. By F. LAGRANGE. Crown 8vo. 5s. (International Scientific Series.)

LANDON. SCHOOL MANAGEMENT : including a General View of the Work of Education, Organisation, and Discipline. By JOSEPH LANDON. Seventh Edition. Crown 8vo. 6s. (Education Library.)

LUCKES. LECTURES ON GENERAL NURSING, Delivered to the Probationers of the London Hospital Training School for Nurses. By EVA C. E. LUCKES. Third Edition. Crown 8vo. 2s. 6d.

LYSCHINSKA and MONTEFIORE. FROEBEL'S ETHICAL TEACHING: Two Essays. By M. J. LYSCHINSKA and T. G. MONTEFIORE. Fcap. 8vo. 2s. 6d.

MAHAFFY. OLD GREEK EDUCATION. By Prof. MAHAFFY. Second Edition. 3s. 6d. (Educational Library.)

MAGNUS. INDUSTRIAL EDUCATION. By Sir PHILIP MAGNUS. 6s. (Education Library.)

MASON. HOME EDUCATION : a Course of Lectures to Ladies. By CHARLOTTE M. MASON. Crown 8vo. 3s. 6d.

MEYER. ORGANS OF SPEECH AND THEIR APPLICATION IN THE FORMATION OF ARTICULATE SOUNDS. By G. HERMANN VON MEYER. With 47 Woodcuts. Crown 8vo. 5s. (International Scientific Series.)

MORRIS. SIMPLIFIED GRAMMAR OF THE TELUGU GRAMMAR. [By HENRY MORRIS. With Map. Crown 8vo. 10s. 6d.

PLUMPTRE. KING'S COLLEGE LECTURES ON ELOCU-
TION; or, The Physiology and Culture of Voice and Speech, and
the Expression of the Emotions by Language, Countenance, and
Gesture. To which is added a Special Lecture on the Causes and
Cure of the Impediments of Speech. By CHARLES JOHN PLUMPTRE,
Lecturer at King's College, London. Fourth and Greatly Enlarged
Illustrated Edition. 8vo. 15s.

PUBLIC SCHOOLS (OUR). ETON, HARROW, WINCHESTER,
RUGBY, WESTMINSTER, MARLBOROUGH, and the CHARTER-
HOUSE. Crown 8vo. 6s.

PURITZ. CODE-BOOK OF GYMNASTIC EXERCISES. By
LUDWIG PURITZ. Translated by O. KNOFE and J. W. MAC-
QUEEN. 32mo. Boards. 1s. 6d.

RAVENSTEIN and HULLEY. THE GYMNASIUM AND ITS
FITTINGS. By E. G. RAVENSTEIN and JOHN HULLEY. With
Illustrations. 8vo. 2s. 6d.

RHYS. LECTURES ON WELSH PHILOLOGY. By JOHN RHYS.
Second Edition. Crown 8vo. 15s.

RICHTER. CHEMISTRY OF THE CARBON COMPOUNDS;
or, Organic Chemistry. By Prof. VICTOR VON RICHTER, University of Breslau. Authorised Translation by EDGAR F. SMITH,
Professor of Chemistry. From the Sixth German Edition. Crown
8vo. Illustrated. 20s.

"We have no English equivalent to Richter. . . . Every chemist will use it."—
Lancet.
"A carefully-written exhaustive treatise, brought well up to date."—*British Medical Journal.*

RICHTER. TEXT-BOOK OF INORGANIC CHEMISTRY.
By Prof. VICTOR VON RICHTER, University of Breslau. Authorised
Translation by EDGAR F. SMITH, Professor of Chemistry. From
the Fourth German Edition. With 89 Woodcuts and Coloured
Lithographic Plate of Spectra. Crown 8vo. 8s. 6d.

SAYCE. INTRODUCTION TO THE SCIENCE OF LAN-
GUAGE. By A. H. SAYCE. New and Cheaper Edition. 2 vols.
Crown 8vo. 9s.

SAYWELL. HANDBOOK OF COUNTY DIALECTS. By J. L.
SAYWELL. Crown 8vo. 5s.

SCHAIBLE. SYSTEMATIC TRAINING OF THE BODY. By
C. H. SCHAIBLE. Crown 8vo. 5s.

SCHLEICHER. COMPARATIVE GRAMMAR OF THE INDO-
EUROPEAN, SANSKRIT, GREEK, and LATIN LANGUAGES.
By AUGUST SCHLEICHER. From the Third German Edition, by H.
BENDALL. 8vo. 13s. 6d.

SELBY. SHAKESPEARE CLASSICAL DICTIONARY; or,
Mythological Allusions in the Plays of Shakespeare Explained. By
H. M. SELBY. Fcap. 8vo. 1s.

SMITH. GLOSSARY OF TERMS AND PHRASES. Edited by H. Percy Smith and others. Cheaper Edition. Medium 8vo. 3s. 6d.

SPECIMENS OF ENGLISH PROSE STYLE FROM MALORY TO MACAULAY. Selected and Annotated with an Introductory Essay by George Saintsbury. Large crown 8vo, printed on hand-made paper. Vellum, 15s. Parchment antique or cloth, 12s.

STRECKER. TEXT-BOOK OF ORGANIC CHEMISTRY. By Adolph Strecker. Edited by Professor Wislicenus. Translated and Edited with extensive Additions by W. R. Hodgkinson and A. J. Greenaway. Second and Cheaper Edition. 8vo. 12s. 6d.

TRENCH. ON THE STUDY OF WORDS. By Archbishop Trench. Twenty-first Edition. Revised by A. L. Mayhew. 12mo. 5s.

TRENCH. ENGLISH PAST AND PRESENT. By Archbishop Trench. Fourteenth Edition. Revised by A. L. Mayhew. 12mo. 5s.

WHITNEY. LANGUAGE AND ITS STUDY, WITH SPECIAL Reference to the Indo-European Family of Languages. By Prof. W. D. Whitney. Edited by R. Morris. Second Edition. Crown 8vo. 5s.

WHITNEY. LIFE AND GROWTH OF LANGUAGE. By Prof. W. D. Whitney. Fifth Edition. Crown 8vo. 5s.

WHITNEY. ESSENTIALS OF ENGLISH GRAMMARS. By Prof. W. D. Whitney. Second Edition. Crown 8vo. 3s. 6d.

WHITNEY. LANGUAGE AND THE STUDY OF LANGUAGE. By Prof. W. D. Whitney. Fourth Edition. Crown 8vo. 10s. 6d.

WEDGWOOD. DICTIONARY OF ENGLISH ETYMOLOGY. By H. Wedgwood, M.A. Third Edition, Revised and Enlarged. With Introduction on the Origin of Language. Fourth Edition. 8vo. £1, 1s.

WEDGWOOD. CONTESTED ETYMOLOGIES IN THE DICTIONARY OF THE REV. W. W. SKEAT. By H. Wedgwood. Crown 8vo. 5s.

WIEBÉ. THE PARADISE OF CHILDHOOD. A Manual for Self-Instruction in Friedrich Froebel's Educational Principles, and a Practical Guide to Kinder-Gartners. By Edward Wiebé. With Seventy-four Plates of Illustrations. 4to. Paper. 7s. 6d.

YOUMANS. FIRST BOOK OF BOTANY, designed to Cultivate the Observing Powers of Children. By Eliza A. Youmans. With 300 Engravings. New and Cheaper Edition. Crown 8vo. 2s. 6d.

FRENCH.

AHN. NEW, PRACTICAL, AND EASY METHOD OF LEARNING THE FRENCH LANGUAGE. By Dr. F. Ahn First Course. 12mo. 1s. 6d. Second Course. 12mo. 1s. 6d. The Two Courses in 1 vol. 12mo. 3s.

AHN. NEW, PRACTICAL, AND EASY METHOD OF LEARNING THE FRENCH LANGUAGE. Third Course, containing a French Reader, with Notes and Vocabulary. By H. W. EHRLICH. 12mo. 1s. 6d.

BELLOWS. TOUS LES VERBES. Conjugations of all the Verbs in the French and English Languages. By JOHN BELLOWS. Also a New Table of Equivalent Values of French and English Money, Weights and Measures. Second Edition. 32mo, sewed. 6d.

BELLOWS. DICTIONARY FOR THE POCKET. French and English—English and French. Both divisions on same page. By JOHN BELLOWS. Masculine and Feminine Words shown by distinguishing Types, Conjugations of all the Verbs, *Liaison* marked in French Part, and Hints to Aid Pronunciation, together with Tables and Maps. Second Edition. 32mo. Roan tuck, 10s. 6d.; morocco tuck, 12s. 6d.

BRETTE and THOMAS. FRENCH EXAMINATION PAPERS, Set at the University of London from 1839 to January 1888. Compiled and Edited by the Rev. P. H. ERNEST BRETTE, B.D., Head Master of the French School, Christ's Hospital, London; Examiner in the University of London; at Eton College, &c., &c.; and FERDINAND THOMAS, B.A., B.Sc., Late Assistant Examiner in the University of London.

PART I.—MATRICULATION EXAMINATIONS, JULY 1853 to JANUARY 1888. Crown 8vo. 3s. 6d. Key, 5s.

In the Key all the Extracts from the Writings of French Authors are translated into English, and all the Questions on Grammar, Idiom, and Elementary Etymology are fully answered.

PART II.—FIRST B.A. (or INTERMEDIATE IN ARTS) and B.A. PASS EXAMINATIONS; Examinations for Honours (Intermediate in Arts and B.A.); and for Certificates of Higher Proficiency—M.A. (Branch IV.), and D. Litt. Examinations. Crown 8vo. 7s.

CASSAL. GLOSSARY OF IDIOMS, GALLICISMS, and other Difficulties contained in the Senior Course of the Modern French Reader. With Short Notices of the most important French Writers and Historical or Literary Characters, and Hints as to the Works to be Read or Studied. By CHARLES CASSAL, LL.D. 12mo. 2s. 6d.

CASSAL and KARCHER. LITTLE FRENCH READER (THE). Extracted from "The Modern French Reader." Edited by Professor C. CASSAL, LL.B., and Professor T. KARCHER, LL.B. With a New System of Conjugating the French Verbs, by Professor CASSAL. Fourth Edition. Crown 8vo. 2s.

CASSAL and KARCHER. MODERN FRENCH READER (THE). Prose. Junior Course. Edited by C. CASSAL, LL.D., and THEODORE KARCHER, LL.B. Seventh Edition. Crown 8vo. 2s. 6d.

CASSAL and KARCHER. MODERN FRENCH READER
(THE). Senior Course. Edited by C. CASSAL, LL.D., and THEO-
DORE KARCHER, LL.B. Third Edition. Crown 8vo. 4s. With
Glossary, 6s.

EHRLICH. FRENCH READER. With Notes and Vocabulary.
By H. W. EHRLICH. 12mo. 1s. 6d.

FRUSTON. ÉCHO FRANÇAIS. A Practical Guide to French
Conversation. By F. DE LA FRUSTON. With a Complete Vocabulary. Second Edition. Crown 8vo. 3s.

KARCHER. QUESTIONNAIRE FRANÇAIS. Questions on
French Grammar, Idiomatic Difficulties, and Military Expressions.
By THEODORE KARCHER, LL.B. Fourth Edition, greatly Enlarged.
Crown 8vo. 4s. 6d. Interleaved with writing paper, 5s. 6d.

LARMOYER. PRACTICAL FRENCH GRAMMAR. By
MORTIMER DE LARMOYER, Professor of the French Language and
Literature at the Crystal Palace School. Two Parts. Crown 8vo.
3s. 6d. each.

LE-BRUN. MATERIALS FOR TRANSLATING FROM ENG-
LISH INTO FRENCH. Being a Short Essay on Translation,
followed by a Graduated Selection in Prose and Verse. By L. LE-
BRUN. Sixth Edition. Revised and Corrected by HENRY VAN
LAUN. Crown 8vo. 4s. 6d.

MARMONTEL. BÉLISAIRE. Par J. F. MARMONTEL. With
Introduction by the Rev. P. H. E. BRETTE and Professors CASSAL
and KARCHER. Nouvelle Edition. 12mo. 2s. 6d.

NOTLEY. COMPARATIVE GRAMMAR OF THE FRENCH,
ITALIAN, SPANISH, AND PORTUGUESE LANGUAGES. With
a Copious Vocabulary. By EDWIN A. NOTLEY. Oblong 12mo.
7s. 6d.

NUGENT'S IMPROVED FRENCH AND ENGLISH AND
ENGLISH AND FRENCH POCKET DICTIONARY. Par SMITH.
24mo. 3s.

POCKET DICTIONARY OF THE ENGLISH AND FRENCH
LANGUAGES. Two Parts bound in 1 vol. 18mo. 5s.

ROCHE. FRENCH GRAMMAR for the Use of English Students,
adopted for the Public Schools by the Imperial Council of Public
Instruction. By A. ROCHE. Crown 8vo. 3s.

ROCHE. PROSE AND POETRY. Select Pieces from the Best
English Authors, for Reading, Composition, and Translation. By
A. ROCHE. Second Edition. Fcap. 8vo. 2s. 6d.

SIMONNÉ. METODO PARA APRENDER A LEER, Escribir y hablir el Frances, segun el verdadero sistema de Ollendorf; ordenado en lecciones progresivas, consistiendo de ejercicios orales y escritos; enriquecido de le pronunciacion figurada como se estila en la conversacion; y de un Apéndice abrazando las reglas de la sintáxis la formacion de los verbos regulares, y la conjugacion de los irregulares. Por TEODORO SIMONNÉ, Professor de Lenguas. Crown 8vo. 6s. Key, 3s. 6d.

THÉÂTRE FRANÇAIS MODERNE. A Selection of Modern French Plays. Edited by the Rev. P. H. E. BRETTE, B.D.; C. CASSAL, LL.D.; and TH. KARCHER, LL.B.

First Series, in 1 vol. crown 8vo. 6s. Containing—
CHARLOTTE CORDAY. A Tragedy. By F. PONSARD.
DIANE. A Drama in Verse. By EMILE AUGIER.
LE VOYAGE À DIEPPE. A Comedy in Prose. By WAFFLARD and FULGENCE.

Second Series, crown 8vo. 6s. Containing—
MOLIÈRE. A Drama in Prose. By GEORGE SAND.
LES ARISTOCRATIES. A Comedy in Verse. By ÉTIENNE ARAGO.

Third Series, crown 8vo. 6s. Containing—
LES FAUX BONSHOMMES. A Comedy. By THÉODORE BARRIÈRE and ERNEST CAPENDU.
L'HONNEUR ET L'ARGENT. A Comedy. By F. PONSARD.

VAN LAUN. GRAMMAR OF THE FRENCH LANGUAGE. In Three Parts. Parts I. and II.—Accidence and Syntax. By H. VAN LAUN. Nineteenth Edition. Crown 8vo. 4s. Part III.—Exercises. Eighteenth Edition. Crown 8vo. 3s. 6d.

WELLER. AN IMPROVED DICTIONARY. English and French, and French and English, including Technical, Scientific, Legal, Commercial, Naval, and Military Terms, Vocabularies of Engineering, &c., Railway Terms, Steam Navigation, Geographical Names, Ancient Mythology, Classical Antiquity, and Christian Names in present use. By E. WELLER. Third Edition. Royal 8vo. 7s. 6d.

FRISIAN.

CUMMINS. GRAMMAR OF THE OLD FRIESIC LANGUAGE. By A. H. CUMMINS, A.M. Crown 8vo. 1887. 6s.

GERMAN.

AHN. PRACTICAL GRAMMAR OF THE GERMAN LANGUAGE, with a Grammatical Index and Glossary of all the German Words. By Dr. F. AHN. A New Edition, containing numerous Additions, Alterations, and Improvements. By DAWSON W. TURNER, D.C.L., and Prof. F. L. WEINMANN. Crown 8vo. 3s. 6d.

12   *A Catalogue of Educational Works.*

AHN. NEW, PRACTICAL, AND EASY METHOD OF LEARNING THE GERMAN LANGUAGE. By Dr. F. AHN. First and Second Course. In 1 volume. 12mo. 3s. Key, 8d.

AHN. MANUAL OF GERMAN CONVERSATION; or, Vade Mecum for English Travellers. By Dr. F. AHN. Second Edition. 12mo. 1s. 6d.

APEL. PROSE SPECIMENS FOR TRANSLATION INTO GERMAN, with Copious Vocabularies. By H. APEL. 12mo. 4s. 6d.

BENEDIX. DER VETTER. Comedy in Three Acts. By RODERICH BENEDIX. With Grammatical and Explanatory Notes by F. WEINMANN, German Master at the Royal Institution School, Liverpool, and G. ZIMMERMANN, Teacher of Modern Languages. 12mo. 2s. 6d.

DUSAR. GRAMMAR OF THE GERMAN LANGUAGE; with Exercises. By P. FRIEDRICH DUSAR, First German Master in the Military Department of Cheltenham College. Second Edition. Crown 8vo. 4s. 6d.

DUSAR. GRAMMATICAL COURSE OF THE GERMAN LANGUAGE. By P. FRIEDRICH DUSAR. Second Edition. Crown 8vo. 3s. 6d.

FRIEDRICH. PROGRESSIVE GERMAN READER. With Copious Notes to the First Part. By P. FRIEDRICH. Second Edition. Crown 8vo. 4s. 6d.

FRŒMBLING. GRADUATED GERMAN READER. Consisting of a Selection from the most Popular Writers, arranged progressively; with a complete Vocabulary for the First Part. By FRIEDRICH OTTO FRŒMBLING, Ph.D. Eighth Edition. 12mo. 3s. 6d.

FRŒMBLING. GRADUATED EXERCISES FOR TRANSLATION INTO GERMAN. Consisting of Extracts from the best English Authors, arranged progressively; with an Appendix, containing Idiomatic Notes. By FRIEDRICH OTTO FRŒMBLING, Ph.D., Principal German Master at the City of London School. Crown 8vo. With Notes, 4s. 6d. Without Notes, 4s.

LANGE. GERMAN PROSE WRITING. Comprising English Passages for Translation into German. Selected from Examination Papers of the University of London, the College of Preceptors, London, and the Royal Military Academy, Woolwich, arranged progressively, with Notes and Theoretical as well as Practical Treatises on Themes for the Writing of Essays. By F. K. W. LANGE, Ph.D., Assistant German Master, Royal Academy, Woolwich; Examiner, Royal College of Preceptors, London. Crown 8vo. 4s.

LANGE. GERMANIA. A German Reading-Book, arranged Progressively. By FRANZ K. W. LANGE, Ph.D. Part I.—Anthology of German Prose and Poetry, with Vocabulary and Biographical Notes. 8vo. 3s. 6d. Part II.—Essays on German History and Institutions. With Notes. 8vo. 3s. 6d. Parts I. and II. together, 5s. 6d.

LANGE. GERMAN GRAMMAR PRACTICE. By F. K. W. LANGE, Ph.D., &c. Crown 8vo. 1s. 6d.

LANGE. COLLOQUIAL GERMAN GRAMMAR. With Special Reference to the Anglo-Saxon Element in the English Language. By F. K. W. LANGE, Ph.D., &c. Crown 8vo. 4s. 6d.

POCKET-DICTIONARY OF THE ENGLISH AND GERMAN LANGUAGES. Two Parts bound in 1 vol. 18mo. 4s.

SINCLAIR. GERMAN VOCABULARY OF SOME OF THE MINOR DIFFICULTIES IN THE GERMAN LANGUAGE, and Easy Conversations. By F. SINCLAIR. Crown 8vo. 2s.

WOLFRAM. DEUTSCHES ECHO. The German Echo. A Faithful Mirror of German Conversation. By LUDWIG WOLFRAM. With a Vocabulary by HENRY P. SKELTON. Sixth Revised Edition. Crown 8vo. 3s.

GREEK.

ÆSCHYLUS. SEVEN PLAYS. Translated into English Verse by LEWIS CAMPBELL. Crown 8vo. 7s. 6d.

ARISTOTLE. THE NICOMACHEAN ETHICS OF ARISTOTLE. Translated by F. H. PETERS. Third Edition. Crown 8vo. 6s.

CONTOPOULOS. LEXICON OF MODERN GREEK-ENGLISH AND ENGLISH-MODERN GREEK. By N. CONTOPOULOS. 2 vols. 8vo. 27s.

CONTOPOULOS. HANDBOOK OF ENGLISH AND GREEK DIALOGUES AND CORRESPONDENCE, with a Short Guide to the Antiquities of Athens. By N. CONTOPOULOS. Crown 8vo. 2s. 6d.

GELDART. GUIDE TO MODERN GREEK. By E. M. GELDART, M.A. Post 8vo. 7s. 6d. Key, 2s. 6d.

GELDART. SIMPLIFIED GRAMMAR OF MODERN GREEK. By E. M. GELDART, M.A. Crown 8vo. 2s. 6d.

HOMER'S ILIAD. Greek Text, with Translation by J. G. CORDERY. 2 vols. 8vo. 14s. Cheap Edition (translation only). Crown 8vo. 5s.

LASCARIDES. COMPREHENSIVE PHRASEOLOGICAL ENGLISH - ANCIENT AND MODERN GREEK LEXICON. Founded upon a Manuscript of G. P. LASCARIDES, Esq., and compiled by L. MYRIANTHEUS, Ph.D. 2 vols. Fcap. 8vo. £1, 10s.

SOPHOCLES. THE SEVEN PLAYS. Translated into English verse by LEWIS CAMPBELL. Crown 8vo. 7s. 6d.

HUNGARIAN.

SINGER. SIMPLIFIED GRAMMAR OF THE HUNGARIAN LANGUAGE. By IGNATIUS SINGER, of Buda-Pesth. Crown 8vo. 4s. 6d.

INTERNATIONAL LANGUAGES.

SPRAGUE. THE INTERNATIONAL LANGUAGE HANDBOOK OF VOLAPÜK. By CHARLES E. SPRAGUE, Member of the Academy of Volapük, President of the Institute of Accounts, U.S. Crown 8vo. 5s.

WOOD. DICTIONARY OF VOLAPÜK. Volapük-English and English-Volapük. By M. M. WOOD, M.D., Captain and Assistant-Surgeon, United States Army, Volapükatidel e cif. Crown 8vo. 10s. 6d.

Volapük has obtained a footing of its own among the speakers of twenty-one different tongues, and its adherents are numbered by hundreds of thousands.

ITALIAN.

AHN. NEW, PRACTICAL, AND EASY METHOD OF LEARNING THE ITALIAN LANGUAGE. By Dr. F. AHN. First and Second Course. Thirteenth Issue. 12mo. 3s. 6d.

CAMERINI. L'ECO ITALIANO. A Practical Guide to Italian Conversation. By EUGENE CAMERINI. With a Complete Vocabulary. Second Edition. Crown 8vo. 4s. 6d.

LANARI. COLLECTION OF ITALIAN AND ENGLISH DIALOGUES ON GENERAL SUBJECTS. For the Use of those Desirous of Speaking the Italian Language Correctly. Preceded by a Brief Treatise on the Pronunciation of the same. By A. LANARI. 12mo. 3s. 6d.

MILLHOUSE. MANUAL OF ITALIAN CONVERSATION, for the Use of Schools and Travellers. By JOHN MILLHOUSE. New Edition. 18mo. 2s.

MILLHOUSE. NEW ENGLISH AND ITALIAN PRONOUNCING AND EXPLANATORY DICTIONARY. By JOHN MILLHOUSE. Vol. I. English-Italian. Vol. II. Italian-English. Sixth Edition. 2 vols. Square 8vo. 12s.

NOTLEY. COMPARATIVE GRAMMAR OF THE FRENCH, ITALIAN, SPANISH, AND PORTUGUESE LANGUAGES. With a Copious Vocabulary. By EDWIN A. NOTLEY. Oblong 12mo. 7s. 6d.

POCKET-DICTIONARY OF THE ENGLISH AND ITALIAN LANGUAGES. Two Parts bound in 1 vol. 18mo. 5s.

TOSCANI. ITALIAN CONVERSATIONAL COURSE. A New Method of Teaching the Italian Language, both Theoretically and Practically. By GIOVANNI TOSCANI, late Professor of the Italian Language and Literature in Queen's College, London, &c. Fifth Edition. 12mo. 5s.

TOSCANI. ITALIAN READING COURSE. Comprehending Specimens in Prose and Poetry of the most distinguished Italian Writers, with Biographical Notices, Explanatory Notes, and Rules on Prosody. By G. TOSCANI. 12mo. With Table of Verbs. 4s. 6d.

LATIN.

HORATIUS FLACCUS (Q.) OPERA. Edited by F. A. CORNISH, with Frontispiece. Elzevir 8vo. (Parchment Library.) Vellum, 7s. 6d. Parchment or cloth, 6s.

IHNE. LATIN GRAMMAR FOR BEGINNERS, on Ahn's System. By W. H. IHNE, late Principal of Carlton Terrace School, Liverpool. Crown 8vo. 3s.

LEWIS. THE LETTERS OF PLINY THE YOUNGER. Translated by J. D. LEWIS, M.A., Trinity College, Cambridge. Post 8vo. 5s.

ORIENTAL.

ASTON. GRAMMAR OF THE JAPANESE WRITTEN LANGUAGE. By W. G. ASTON. Second Edition. 8vo. 28s.

ASTON. GRAMMAR OF THE JAPANESE SPOKEN LANGUAGE. By W. G. ASTON. Fourth Edition. Crown 8vo. 12s.

BALLANTYNE. FIRST LESSONS IN SANSKRIT GRAMMAR. By J. R. BALLANTYNE. Fourth Edition. 8vo. 3s. 6d.

BALLANTYNE. ELEMENTS OF HINDI AND BRAJ BHAKHA GRAMMAR, compiled for the East India College at Haileybury. By J. R. BALLANTYNE. Second Edition. Crown 8vo. 5s.

BEAMES. OUTLINES OF INDIAN PHILOLOGY. With a Map showing the Distribution of Indian Languages. By JOHN BEAMES. Enlarged Edition. Crown 8vo. 5s.

BEAMES. COMPARATIVE GRAMMAR OF THE MODERN ARYAN LANGUAGES OF INDIA (Hindi, Panjabi, Sindhi, Gujarati, Marathi, Oriya, and Bengali). By JOHN BEAMES. 3 vols. 8vo. 16s. each.

BELLOWS. ENGLISH OUTLINE VOCABULARY for the Use of Students of the Chinese, Japanese, and other Languages. By JOHN BELLOWS. Second Edition. Royal 8vo. 10s. 6d.

BENFEY. GRAMMAR OF THE SANSKRIT LANGUAGE, for the Use of Early Students. By THEODOR BENFEY. Second Edition. Royal 8vo. 10s. 6d.

BENTLEY. DICTIONARY AND GRAMMAR OF THE KONGO LANGUAGE as spoken at San Salvador, West Africa. By W. H. BENTLEY. 8vo. 21s.

BERTIN. ABRIDGED GRAMMARS OF THE LANGUAGE OF THE CUNEIFORM INSCRIPTIONS. By GEORGE BERTIN. Crown 8vo. 5s.

CALDWELL. COMPARATIVE GRAMMAR OF THE DRAVIDIAN OR SOUTH INDIAN FAMILY OF LANGUAGES. By BISHOP R. CALDWELL. Enlarged Edition. 8vo. 28s.

CHAMBERLAIN. ROMANISED JAPANESE READER, consisting of Japanese Anecdotes and Maxims, with English Translations and Notes. By BASIL CHAMBERLAIN. 12mo. 6s.

CHAMBERLAIN. HANDBOOK OF COLLOQUIAL JAPANESE. By BASIL CHAMBERLAIN. 8vo. 12s. 6d.

CHAMBERLAIN. SIMPLIFIED JAPANESE GRAMMAR. By BASIL CHAMBERLAIN. Crown 8vo. 5s.

CHILDERS. PALI-ENGLISH DICTIONARY. With Sanskrit Equivalents. By R. C. CHILDERS. Imperial 8vo. £3, 3s.

COWELL. SHORT INTRODUCTION TO THE ORDINARY PRAKRIT OF THE SANSKRIT DRAMAS. By E. B. COWELL. Crown 8vo. 3s. 6d.

COWELL. PRAKRITA-PRAKASA : or, The Prakrit Grammar of Vararuchi, with the Commentary (Manorama) of Bhamaha. By E. B. COWELL. 8vo. 14s.

CRAVEN. POPULAR ENGLISH-HINDUSTANI AND HINDUSTANI-ENGLISH DICTIONARY IN ROMAN CHARACTERS. By T. CRAVEN. Second Edition. 12mo. 3s. 6d.'

CUST. MODERN LANGUAGES OF THE EAST INDIES. By R. CUST. With Two Language Maps. Post 8vo. (Trübner's Oriental Series.) 7s. 6d.

CUST. SKETCH OF THE MODERN LANGUAGES OF AFRICA. By R. CUST. With Language Map and 31 Portraits. 2 vols. Post 8vo. (Trübner's Oriental Series.) 18s.

DOUGLAS. CHINESE LANGUAGE AND LITERATURE. By Prof. R. K. DOUGLAS. Crown 8vo 5s.

DOWSON. GRAMMAR OF THE URDU OR HINDUSTANI LANGUAGE. By JOHN DOWSON. Second Edition Crown 8vo. 10s. 6d.

DOWSON. HINDUSTANI EXERCISE BOOK. Passages and Extracts for Translation into Hindūstānī. By JOHN DOWSON. Crown 8vo. 2s. 6d.

DOWSON. CLASSICAL DICTIONARY OF HINDU MYTHOLOGY and HISTORY, GEOGRAPHY and LITERATURE. By JOHN DOWSON. Post 8vo. (Trübner's Oriental Series.) 16s.

DUKA. ESSAY ON THE BRAHUI GRAMMAR. By THEODORE DUKA. 8vo. 3s. 6d.'

EDGREN. COMPENDIOUS SANSKRIT GRAMMAR. With a Brief Sketch of Scenic Prakrit. "By H.'EDGREN. Crown 8v 10s. 6d.

EDKINS. CHINA'S PLACE IN PHILOLOGY. An Attempt to Show that the Languages of Europe and Asia have a Common Origin. By F. EDKINS, D.D. Crown 8vo. 10s. 6d.

EDKINS. THE EVOLUTION OF THE CHINESE LANGUAGE. By F. EDKINS, D.D. 8vo. 4s. 6d.

EDKINS. INTRODUCTION TO THE STUDY OF THE CHINESE CHARACTERS. By F. EDKINS, D.D Royal 8vo. 18s.

FINN. PERSIAN FOR TRAVELLERS. By ALEXANDER FINN. Oblong 32mo. 5s.

HEPBURN. JAPANESE AND ENGLISH DICTIONARY. By J. C. HEPBURN. Second Edition. Imperial 8vo. 18s.

HEPBURN. JAPANESE-ENGLISH AND ENGLISH-JAPANESE DICTIONARY. By J. C. HEPBURN. Abridged by the Author. Square 12mo. 14s.

HEPBURN. JAPANESE-ENGLISH AND ENGLISH-JAPANESE DICTIONARY. By J. C. HEPBURN. Third Edition. 8vo. Half morocco. Cloth sides. £1, 10s.,

JÆSCHKE. TIBETAN GRAMMAR. By H. A. JÆSCHKE. Prepared by Dr. H. WENZEL. Second Edition. Crown 8vo. 5s.

JÆSCHKE. TIBETAN-ENGLISH DICTIONARY. With Special Reference to the Prevailing Dialects. To which is added an English-Tibetan Vocabulary. By H. A. JÆSCHKE. Imperial 8vo. £1, 10s.

KOLBE. A LANGUAGE-STUDY BASED ON BANTU; or, An Inquiry into the Laws of Root-Formation. By F. W. KOLBE. 8vo. 6s.

KRAPF. DICTIONARY OF THE SUAHILI LANGUAGE. By L. KRAPF. 8vo. 30s.

MAXWELL. MANUAL OF THE MALAY LANGUAGE. By W. E. MAXWELL. Second Edition. Crown 8vo. 7s. 6d.

MOCKLER. GRAMMAR OF THE BALOOCHEE LANGUAGE, as it is Spoken in Makran (Ancient Gedrosia), in the Persia-Arabic and Roman Characters. By E. MOCKLER. Fcap. 8vo. 5s.

MÜLLER. OUTLINE DICTIONARY FOR THE USE OF MISSIONARIES, EXPLORERS, AND STUDENTS OF LANGUAGE. By F. MAX MÜLLER. 12mo. Morocco. 7s. 6d.

MÜLLER. SIMPLIFIED GRAMMAR OF THE PALI LANGUAGE. By E. MÜLLER. Crown 8vo. 7s. 6d.

NEWMAN. HANDBOOK OF MODERN ARABIC. By F. W. NEWMAN. Post 8vo. 6s.

NEWMAN. DICTIONARY OF MODERN ARABIC (ANGLO-ARABIC AND ARABO-ENGLISH). By F. W. NEWMAN. 2 vols. Crown 8vo. £1, 1s.

PALMER. ENGLISH-PERSIAN DICTIONARY, with Simplified Grammar of the Persian Language. By E. H. PALMER. Royal 16mo. 10s. 6d.

PALMER. PERSIAN-ENGLISH DICTIONARY. By E. H. PALMER. Second Edition. Royal 16mo. 10s. 6d.

PALMER. SIMPLIFIED GRAMMAR OF HINDUSTANI, PERSIAN, AND ARABIC. By E. H. PALMER. Second Edition. Crown 8vo. 5s.

PARKER. CONCISE GRAMMAR OF THE MALAGASY LANGUAGE. By G. W. PARKER. Crown 8vo. 5s.

PENRICE. DICTIONARY AND GLOSSARY OF THE KOR-AN. With copious Grammatical References and Explanations of the Text. By JOHN PENRICE. 4to. 21s.

PRATT. GRAMMAR AND DICTIONARY OF THE SAMOAN LANGUAGE. By GEORGE PRATT. Second Edition. Crown 8vo. 18s.

ROBERTS. A GRAMMAR OF THE KHASSI LANGUAGE, for the Use of Schools, Native Students, Officers, and English Residents. By H. ROBERTS. Crown 8vo. 10s. 6d.

SALMONÉ. ARABIC-ENGLISH DICTIONARY, comprising about 120,000 Arabic Words, with English Index of about 50,000 Words. By H. A. SALMONE. 2 vols. Post 8vo. Half-bound. 36s.

SAYCE. ASSYRIAN GRAMMAR, for Comparative Purposes. By A. H. SAYCE. Crown 8vo. 7s. 6d.

TARRING. ELEMENTARY TURKISH GRAMMAR. By C. J. TARRING. Crown 8vo. 6s.

TISDALL. SIMPLIFIED GRAMMAR AND READING-BOOK OF THE PANJĀBĪ LANGUAGE. By W. ST. CLAIR TISDALL. Crown 8vo. 7s. 6d.

TISDALL. SIMPLIFIED GRAMMAR OF THE GUJARĀTĪ LANGUAGE, together with a Short Reading-Book and Vocabulary. By W. ST. CLAIR TISDALL. Crown 8vo.

WHITNEY. SANSKRIT GRAMMAR, including both the Classical Language and the Older Dialects of Veda and Brahmana. By Prof. W. L WHITNEY. Second Edition. 8vo. 12s.

WILLIAMS. SYLLABIC DICTIONARY OF THE CHINESE LANGUAGE: Arranged according to the Wu-Fang Yuen Yin, with the Pronunciation of the Characters as heard in Pekin, Canton, Amoy, and Shanghai. By S. WELLS WILLIAMS. New Edition. 4to. Half calf. £5, 5s.

POLISH.

BARANOWSKI. SLOWNIK POLSKO-ANGIELSKI OPRACOWANY. Przez J. J. BARANOWSKIEGO, b. Podsekretarza Banku Polskiego. w Warszawie. (Polish-English Lexicon. With Grammatical Rules in Polish.) 16mo. 12s.

BARANOWSKI. ANGLO - POLISH LEXICON. By J. J. BARANOWSKI, formerly Under-Secretary to the Bank of Poland, in Warsaw. (With Grammatical Rules in English, and a Second Part, containing Dialogues, Bills of Exchange, Receipts, Letters, &c.; English and Polish Proverbs, &c.) 16mo. 12s.

MORFILL. SIMPLIFIED GRAMMAR OF THE POLISH LANGUAGE. By W. R. MORFILL, M.A. Crown 8vo. 3s. 6d.

PORTUGUESE.

ANDERSON AND TUGMAN. MERCANTILE CORRESPONDENCE. Containing a Collection of Commercial Letters in Portuguese and English, with their Translation on Opposite Pages, for the Use of Business Men and of Students in either of the Languages, treating in Modern Style of the System of Business in the principal Commercial Cities of the World. Accompanied by *pro forma* Accounts, Sales, Invoices, Bills of Lading, Drafts, &c With an Introduction and Copious Notes. By WILLIAM ANDERSON and JAMES E. TUGMAN. 12mo. 6s.

D'ORSEY. PRACTICAL GRAMMAR OF PORTUGUESE AND ENGLISH. Exhibiting in a Series of Exercises, in Double Translation, the Idiomatic Structure of both Languages, as now Written and Spoken. By the Rev. ALEXANDER J. D. D'ORSEY, B.D., of Corpus Christi College, Cambridge, and Lecturer on Public Reading and Speaking at King's College, London. Fourth Edition. Crown 8vo. 7s.

D'ORSEY. COLLOQUIAL PORTUGUESE; or, Words and Phrases of Everyday Life. Compiled from Dictation and Conversation. For the Use of English Tourists in Portugal, Brazil, Madeira, and the Azores. With a Brief Collection of Epistolary Phrases. By the Rev. A. J. D. D'ORSEY. Fourth Edition. Enlarged crown 8vo. 3s. 6d.

NOTLEY. COMPARATIVE GRAMMAR OF THE FRENCH, ITALIAN, SPANISH, AND PORTUGUESE LANGUAGES. With a Copious Vocabulary. By EDWIN A. NOTLEY. Oblong 12mo. 7s. 6d.

VIEYRA. NEW POCKET - DICTIONARY OF THE PORTUGUESE AND ENGLISH LANGUAGES. In Two Parts: Portuguese - English and English - Portuguese. Abridged from "Vieyra's Dictionary." A New Edition, considerably enlarged and Corrected. 2 vols. Pott 8vo. Bound in leather. 10s.

ROUMANIAN.

*TORCEANU. SIMPLIFIED GRAMMAR OF THE ROUMANIAN LANGUAGE. By R. TORCEANU. Crown 8vo. 5s.

RUSSIAN.

ALEXANDROW. COMPLETE ENGLISH-RUSSIAN AND RUSSIAN-ENGLISH DICTIONARY. By A. ALEXANDROW. 2 vols. 8vo. 40s.

FREETH. CONDENSED RUSSIAN GRAMMAR. For the Use of Staff-Officers and Others. By F. FREETH, B.A., late Classical Scholar of Emmanuel College, Cambridge. Crown 8vo. 3s. 6d.

IVANOFF'S RUSSIAN GRAMMAR. Sixteenth Edition. Translated, Enlarged, and Arranged for Use of Students. By Major W. E. GOWAN. 8vo. 6s.

MAKAROFF. DICTIONNAIRE FRANCAIS-RUSSE ET RUSSE-FRANCAIS. Complet. Composé par N. P. MAKAROFF, Honoré par l'Académie des Sciences d'une Mention Honorable, approuvé par les Comités Scientifiques et adopté dans les Établissements d'Instruction. 2 vols. in 4 parts. Super-royal, 8vo. Half Bound. 40s.

POCKET-DICTIONARY OF THE ENGLISH AND RUSSIAN LANGUAGES. Two Parts bound in 1 vol. 18mo. 5s. 6d.

RIOLA. HOW TO LEARN RUSSIAN. A Manual for Students of Russian, based upon the Ollendorffian System of Teaching Languages, and adapted for Self-Instruction. By HENRY RIOLA, Teacher of the Russian Language. With a Preface by W. R. S. RALSTON, M.A. Fourth Edition. Crown 8vo. 12s. Key to ditto. Crown 8vo. 5s.

RIOLA. GRADUATED RUSSIAN READER. With a Vocabulary of all the Russian Words contained in it. By HENRY RIOLA. Crown 8vo. 10s. 6d.

THOMPSON. DIALOGUES, RUSSIAN AND ENGLISH. Compiled by A. R. THOMPSON, some time Lecturer of the English Language in the University of St. Vladimir, Kieff. Crown 8vo. 5s.

SERBIAN.

MORFILL. SIMPLIFIED GRAMMAR [OF THE SERBIAN LANGUAGE. By W. R. MORFILL, M.A. Crown 8vo. 4s. 6d.

SPANISH.

BUTLER. THE SPANISH TEACHER AND COLLOQUIAL PHRASE-BOOK. An Easy and Agreeable Method of Acquiring a Speaking Knowledge of the Spanish Language. By FRANCIS BUTLER. 18mo. Half-roan. 2s. 6d.

CARRENO. METODO PARA APRENDER A LEER, Escribir y hablar el Inglés segun el sistema de Ollendorff, con un tratado de pronunciacion al principio y un Apendice importante al fin, que sirve de complemento a la obra. Por RAMON PALENZUELA y JUAN DE LA CARRENO. Nueva Edicion, con una Pronunciacion Figurada segun un Sistema Fonografico, por ROBERT GOODACRE. Crown 8vo. 4s. 6d. Key, 3s.

HARTZENBUSCH AND LEMMING. ECO DE MADRID. A Practical Guide to Spanish Conversation. By J. E. HARTZENBUSCH and H. LEMMING. Third Edition. Crown 8vo. 5s.

HARVEY. SIMPLIFIED GRAMMAR OF THE SPANISH LANGUAGE. By W. F. HARVEY, M.A. Crown 8vo. 3s. 6d.

NOTLEY. COMPARATIVE GRAMMAR OF THE FRENCH, ITALIAN, SPANISH, AND PORTUGUESE LANGUAGES. With a Copious Vocabulary. By EDWIN A. NOTLEY. Oblong 12mo. 7s. 6d.

SIMONNÉ. METODO PARA APRENDER A LEERE, scribir y hablar el Frances, segun el verdadero sistema de Ollendorff; ordenado en lecciones progresivas, consistiendo de ejercicios orales y escritos; enriquecido de la pronunciacion figurada como se estila en la conversacion; y de un Apéndice abrazando las reglas de la sintáxis, la formacion de los verbos regulares, y la conjugacion de los irregulares. Por TEODORO SIMONNÉ, Professor de Lenguas. Crown 8vo. 6s. Key, 3s. 6d.

VELASQUEZ and SIMONNÉ. NEW METHOD [OF LEARNING TO READ, WRITE, AND SPEAK THE SPANISH LANGUAGE. Adapted to Ollendorff's System. By M. VELASQUEZ and J. SIMONNÉ. Crown 8vo. 6s. Key, 4s.

VELASQUEZ. DICTIONARY OF THE SPANISH AND ENGLISH LANGUAGES. For the Use of Learners and Travellers. By M. VELASQUEZ DE LA CADENA. In Two Parts. I. Spanish-English; II. English-Spanish. Crown 8vo. 6s.

VELASQUEZ. PRONOUNCING DICTIONARY OF THE SPANISH AND ENGLISH LANGUAGES. Composed from the Dictionaries of the Spanish Academy, Terreros, Salvá, Webster, Worcester, and Walker. In Two Parts. I. Spanish-English; II. English-Spanish. By M. VELASQUEZ DE LA CADENA. Royal 8vo. £1, 4s.

VELASQUEZ. NEW SPANISH READER. Passages from the most approved Authors, in Prose and Verse. Arranged in Progressive Order with Vocabulary By M. VELASQUEZ DE LA CADENA. Crown 8vo. 6s.

VELASQUEZ. AN EASY INTRODUCTION TO SPANISH CONVERSATION, containing all that is necessary to make a Rapid Progress in it. Particularly designed for Persons who have little time to Study, or are their own Instructors. By M. VELASQUEZ DE LA CADENA. New Edition, Revised and Enlarged. 12mo. 2s. 6d.

SWEDISH.

NILSSON, WIDMARK, and COLLIN. ENGLISH-SWEDISH DICTIONARY. Compiled by L. G. NILSSON, P. F. WIDMARK, and A. Z. COLLIN. New Edition. 8vo. 16s.

OMAN. SVENSK-ENGELSK HAND-ORDBOK. (Swedish-English Dictionary.) By F. E. OMAN. Crown 8vo. 8s.

OTTE. SIMPLIFIED GRAMMAR OF THE SWEDISH LANGUAGE. By E. C. OTTÉ. Crown 8vo. 2s. 6d.

POCKET-DICTIONARY OF THE ENGLISH AND SWEDISH LANGUAGES. Two Parts bound in 1 vol. 18mo. 5s. 6d.

TECHNOLOGICAL DICTIONARIES.

EGER. TECHNOLOGICAL DICTIONARY IN THE ENGLISH AND GERMAN LANGUAGES. Edited by GUSTAV EGER, Professor of the Polytechnic School of Darmstadt, and Sworn Translator of the Grand Ducal Ministerial Departments. Technically Revised and Enlarged by OTTO BRANDES, Chemist. Two vols. Royal 8vo. £1, 7s.

KARMARSCH. TECHNOLOGICAL DICTIONARY OF THE TERMS EMPLOYED IN THE ARTS AND SCIENCES; Architecture, Civil, Military, and Naval; Civil Engineering; Mechanics; Machine-Making; Shipbuilding and Navigation; Metallurgy; Artillery; Mathematics; Physics; Chemistry; Mineralogy, &c. With a Preface by Dr. K. KARMARSCH. Third Edition. Three vols

    Vol. I. German-English-French. 8vo. 12s.
    Vol. II. English-German-French. 8vo. 12s.
    Vol. III. French-German-English. 8vo. 15s.

TURKISH.

ARNOLD. A SIMPLE TRANSLITERAL GRAMMAR OF THE TURKISH LANGUAGE. Compiled from Various Sources. With Dialogues and Vocabulary. By Sir EDWIN ARNOLD. Pott 8vo. 2s. 6d.

HOPKINS. ELEMENTARY GRAMMAR OF THE TURKISH LANGUAGE. With a Few Easy Exercises. By F. L. HOPKINS, M.A., Fellow and Tutor of Trinity Hall, Cambridge. Crown 8vo. 3s. 6d.

REDHOUSE. THE TURKISH VADE-MECUM OF OTTOMAN COLLOQUIAL LANGUAGE. Containing a Concise Ottoman Grammar; a Carefully Selected Vocabulary, Alphabetically Arranged, in Two Parts, English-Turkish and Turkish-English; also a Few Familiar Dialogues and Naval and Military Terms. The whole in English Characters, the Pronunciation being Fully Indicated. By J. W. REDHOUSE, M.R.A.S. Third Edition. Fourth Thousand. 32mo. 6s.

REDHOUSE. SIMPLIFIED GRAMMAR OF THE OTTOMAN TURKISH LANGUAGE. By J. W. REDHOUSE, M.R.A.S. Crown 8vo. 10s. 6d.

REDHOUSE. TURKISH AND ENGLISH LEXICON. Showing in English the Signification of the Turkish Terms. By J. W. REDHOUSE, M.R.A.S. Parts I. to VII. Imperial 8vo. Paper covers. £3, 3s.

LONDON : KEGAN PAUL, TRENCH, TRÜBNER, & CO. L^{TD}
    PATERNOSTER HOUSE, CHARING CROSS ROAD.

www.ingramcontent.com/pod-product-compliance
Lightning Source LLC
Chambersburg PA
CBHW021946160426
43195CB00011B/1240